THE MANAGEMENT COACH

Rus Slater

First published in Great Britain in 2014 by Hodder & Stoughton. An Hachette UK company.

First published in US in 2014 by The McGraw-Hill Companies, Inc.

British Library Cataloguing in Publication Data: a catalogue record for this title is available from the British Library.

Library of Congress Catalog Card Number: on file.

10 9 8 7 6 5 4 3 2 1

Paperback ISBN 978 1 471 80156 3

The publisher has used its best endeavours to ensure that any website addresses referred to in this book are correct and active at the time of going to press. However, the publisher and the author have no responsibility for the websites and can make no guarantee that a site will remain live or that the content will remain relevant, decent or appropriate.

The publisher has made every effort to mark as such all words which it believes to be trademarks. The publisher should also like to make it clear that the presence of a word in the book, whether marked or unmarked, in no way affects its legal status as a trademark.

Every reasonable effort has been made by the publisher to trace the copyright holders of material in this book. Any errors or omissions should be notified in writing to the publisher, who will endeavour to rectify the situation for any reprints and future editions.

Typeset by Cenveo® Publisher Services.

Printed and bound in Great Britain by CPI Group (UK) Ltd, Croydon CR0 4YY.

Hodder & Stoughton policy is to use papers that are natural, renewable and recyclable products and made from wood grown in sustainable forests. The logging and manufacturing processes are expected to conform to the environmental regulations of the country of origin.

Hodder & Stoughton Ltd
338 Euston Road
London NW1 3BH
www.hodder.co.uk

Also available in ebook

CONTENTS

MEET THE COACH

Rus Slater is a professional learning and development specialist, business coach and author. As an independent consultant he brings performance improvement to both individuals and organizations, and clients have ranged from multinationals like BP to charities such as Guide Dogs for the Blind. His publications include: *Be a Better Manager In A Week* (Hodder, 2013) and *Dragons' Den: Start Your Own Business* (Collins, 2010).

HOW TO USE THIS BOOK

Welcome to *The Management Coach*. This isn't a book that you just read and then walk away from. The idea is that each section challenges you to reflect, consider and explore; there are exercises and activities (the 'coaching sessions') throughout that will request you to stop and complete them before you move on.

Unlike an e-learning course, it cannot force you; you may chose to skip the coaching sessions and just read on. But if you don't take the time to ponder, to reflect and to investigate your own management preferences, style and behaviours then you will not get the full value of the book.

If you do make that effort, then you will reap the rewards. Or, perhaps more to the point, the people you manage will reap the rewards!

You will find the following features in each chapter:

 **OUTCOMES FROM THIS CHAPTER**

Each chapter starts with a few bullet points detailing the main outcomes of the chapter.

 **COACHING SESSIONS**

These include:

- workplace exercises using the discoveries made from completing a self-assessment
- tables for you to complete
- checklists or tick lists
- forms and worksheets (for recording or challenging beliefs/thoughts)
- questions whose aim is to guide your learning.

ONLINE RESOURCE

These boxes will contain complementary online resources and coaching sessions for you to download free of charge and make use of.

NEXT STEPS

At the end of each chapter you will find a summary of what you have learned and what you have done in the chapter, as well as what comes next.

TAKEAWAYS

Also at the end of each chapter are three or four questions to help you reflect on what you have learned from the chapter and carry that learning forward.

INTRODUCTION TO MANAGEMENT

 OUTCOMES FROM THIS INTRODUCTION

- Begin to think about the nature of management.
- Understand the difference between leadership and management
- Learn about the development of management as a discipline.

Management. It is a word that means different things to different people:

- To some, 'management' is a pejorative term for people who do no work but enjoy long lunches, short careers and large bonuses.

- To others, it is a faceless clique that makes decisions by some sort of black art, but is not made up of human beings who are subject to the same sort of pressures and foibles as the rest of us mere mortals.

- To some, it is an activity: they are involved in the 'management' of inanimate objects rather than people. 'IT management' or 'facilities management' are usually quoted in this area.

- To others still, 'management' may be an abstract activity; fund management or project management are examples of this understanding of the word.

In reality, all forms of management involve intellectual input as well as emotional intelligence; it is almost impossible to 'manage' without interacting with people somewhere along the way.

Having said that, some people barely manage to manage themselves, and if you can't manage yourself, then you are going to find it almost impossible to manage anything else, be it people or resources.

This book will help you:

- to manage yourself as a foundation for managing others, and then...

- to manage others to benefit your own career.

Don't worry, though, the book is not 'The Janet and John Book of Management', which is going to insult your intelligence by starting out with potty-training and your abc. It will, however, challenge you to look at many of the foundation self-management elements, such as working out what you actually want in life and what actually makes you tick. Only through this sort of self-awareness can you become an effective manager and leader of people.

This brings us on to the hoary subject of 'leadership vs. management'. Is there a difference?

What do you think?

COACHING SESSION 1

Leadership vs. management

Take a couple of hours to consider and write out answers to the five questions below.

This is not a test; there are no right answers at the back of the book. It is an exercise in reflection, a way of getting you to ponder on the wider issues so that you can start to manage your own thoughts, philosophy and therefore your reactions and responses to different situations and different people's behaviours.

1. What are the primary characteristics and behaviours of a good manager?

_____

_____

_____

_____

_____

_____

_____

_____

_____

_____

_____

2. What are the primary characteristics and behaviours of a good leader?

_____

_____

_____

_____

_____

_____

_____

_____

_____

3. What makes a person easy to manage?

_____

_____

_____

_____

_____

_____

_____

_____

_____

_____

_____

4. What makes a person a good follower of a leader?

_____

_____

_____

_____

_____

_____

_____

_____

_____

5. What is the difference between 'being managed' and 'being led'?

_____

_____

_____

_____

_____

_____

_____

_____

_____

_____

If you are staring blankly at the questions with no ideas at all, here is a brief list of resources that you may like to look at that may help you to start to crystallize your thinking:

Margot Morrell and Stephanie Capparell, *Shackleton's Way: Leadership Lessons from the Great Antarctic Explorer* (Penguin, 2002)

http://changingminds.org/disciplines/leadership/articles/manager_leader.htm

http://businessballs.com/leadership.htm

THE HISTORY OF MODERN MANAGEMENT AS A DISCIPLINE

Notwithstanding the ancient world's ability to produce major construction projects such as the pyramids, the Colosseum and the aqueducts of the Roman Empire, 'management' as we know it is a pretty modern discipline. Historically, management was mostly a function of people born with something to manage; otherwise the only way to actually generate something to manage was to beat people up and take what they had, thereby accumulating resources. Notwithstanding some warlords in strife-torn nations and a couple of global entrepreneurs, this is no longer seen as a legitimate method of self-promotion.

Prior to the Industrial Revolution, most wealth was generated though agriculture. This required little management: land was tenanted out and the tenant paid a proportion of his (and it was almost exclusively male dominated) income to the landowner. Farms were generally small and very inefficient, supporting, often only just, a large number of labourers. Often people worked for food rather than money, so much of the population existed pretty much at a subsistence level. Few people amassed enough wealth to start employing large numbers of people who needed managing.

With the Industrial Revolution, however, came several major changes (whether you'd call them 'advances' is another matter).

- Business owners had invested large amounts of money in mechanization; they now had shareholders who needed repayment and this meant that the business needed to run at maximum efficiency. The new business owners had little sense of 'noblesse oblige'; they were generally people who had come from backgrounds with little or no wealth and now saw this as an opportunity to 'better' themselves – most had little regard for the people who worked for them.

- There was little change in the average working person; they remained poorly educated and ripe for exploitation. However, for many, the rigours of factory life were still much, much better than the crippling poverty of life as an agricultural labourer or domestic servant.

- For pretty much the first time, standards of productivity could be estimated. In agriculture there were simply too many variables to make much of a sensible plan about most tasks. Tools were expensive and of generally poor quality, and if they broke it could take several days before they got repaired. A factory machine, however, had a given optimum operating speed and output. Production rates could therefore be anticipated and expected. Now the main variable was the people 'serving' the machines. 'Management', as we know it, was born.

Well, it was 'management', Jim, but not as we know it!

There was little or nothing by way of employment legislation or health and safety; business owners could pretty much do as they liked. After all they controlled the means of production, and if workers didn't toe the line, then there was little to stop the employer giving them the sack.

At the same time, the workforce, as mentioned before, were desperate to move away from the land and get jobs in factories, where the wages, while low, were at least regular and paid in cash. Serving the machines was repetitive and tiring, but relatively unskilled. The laws of supply and demand played into the hands of the business owners and this made it even easier to 'manage' the workforce.

'Management' was based on coercion, compulsion and control.

So it remained for some years.

It was the Victorians who began to move management away from these three Cs of coercion, compulsion and control. But only by a little bit.

The morality of the Victorian elite demanded improvements in welfare and working conditions, while at the same time the work ethic (and desire for profit) of the Victorian elite demanded improvements in efficiency and output. This began two differing strands of change in the development of management. A raft of welfare-based laws on such matters as child labour and health and safety began – in a paternalistic way – to slowly erode the business owners' rights to treat their workforce in the same way they treated their machinery. At the same time, 'time and motion' studies began looking into the matters of efficiency and productivity: output was measured in relation to different factors, and optimum conditions were created to make the factories as efficient as possible.

Since the Victorian era, two world wars proved to the working classes that they had intrinsic value in their own right. Subsequent large-scale changes in the concepts of human rights have led to changes and evolution in management. Old-style management by the three Cs has given way, in theory at least, to a more enlightened culture of co-operation, compromise and consensus.

So much for the history lesson, but what value does that give you today as a manager?

THE TWO CULTURES OF MANAGEMENT

If we accept that, in the past, 'management' was based predominantly on

- coercion
- compulsion
- control

...and that managing a twenty-first-century workforce requires more by way of

- co-operation
- compromise
- consensus

...then what are the differences between the characteristics of managers and the managed under the different cultures?

⌯⌯ COACHING SESSION 2

The two cultures of management

Use the grids below to help you to arrive at, and record, your thoughts about the two cultures of management.

In order to manage by coercion, compulsion and control, you will have to have the following characteristics:

Among the managers...	Among the managed...
An innate belief in their right to manage over their workforce	They know their place and are subservient

In order to manage by co-operation, compromise and consensus, you will have to have the following characteristics:

Among the managers…	Among the managed…
Recognition that the job title doesn't mean you are always right	A willingness to make the intellectual effort to contribute

Now take a look at the things you have listed in the 'co-operation, compromise and consensus' table.

1. Do you exhibit all the characteristics you listed in the left-hand column? Rate yourself out of 10, where 0 is 'a total lack of this characteristic' and 10 is 'displayed 100 per cent of the time, with 100 per cent of the people'.

If your score is low, then you are going to find it hard to manage people effectively. The higher your score, the easier you should find it to be a good twenty-first-century manager... unless, you are deluding yourself. You may be able to 'sanity-check' your self-appraisal by getting people who work for you to give you their opinions, but if you have no staff at present then this is not an option and a self-appraisal is the only real option.

2. Do you believe that your people have the characteristics that you have listed in the right-hand column? Rate them out of 10, where 0 is 'a total lack of this characteristic' and 10 is 'displayed 100 per cent of the time'.

If your score is low, then you lack belief in your people's capacity. In this case, you will give yourself little option but to manage by coercion, compulsion and control. And that is actually much harder work!

If you are really struggling with this activity, the table below gives possible answers. They are examples, not a full, comprehensive list of all possible answers. Use them if necessary to kick-start your thinking.

Coercion, compulsion and control

In order to manage by coercion, compulsion and control, managers will have to have the following characteristics:

Among the managers....	Among the managed...
An innate belief in their right to manage over their workforce	They know their place and are subservient
A lack of confidence in the intelligence of the workforce	Don't disagree with the boss (to his/her face)
A belief that knowledge is power, coupled with...	Compliance with rules and orders, no matter how wrong or stupid they are
...a desire to keep power for themselves and not share it	A refusal to show initiative
A willingness or even a desire to be unpopular	A reluctance to attempt to improve processes at work
A willingness or a even a desire to be feared	A reluctance to attempt to better themselves and their lot

(Continued)

Among the managers....	Among the managed...
A 'dog-in-a-manger' approach to getting and keeping the status that goes with rank	A genuine ignorance
A desire to keep people in their place (below me!)	A feigned ignorance
A conviction that they always know best	A willingness to put up with being treated like mushrooms*
A perception that to apologize, ask for help or admit ignorance is a weakness to be hidden	A permanent fear that any spark of initiative or admission of ignorance or a need for support will result in punitive action

* Kept in the metaphorical dark and fed on metaphorical manure

Co-operation, compromise and consensus

In order to manage by co-operation, compromise and consensus, managers will have to have the following characteristics:

Among the managers....	Among the managed...
Recognition that the job title doesn't mean you are always right	A willingness to make the intellectual effort to contribute
A willingness to ask subordinates for their advice and guidance	Act reasonably and not take advantage of the situation
A willingness to ask subordinates for their subjective opinions	Take an interest beyond their job description
An understanding that management brings responsibility, not just perks	Recognize that the boss has lots of different pulls on time and resources and can't always give them what they want
Consideration for their people's private lives and health	Take responsibility for their own development
Preparedness to listen to unsolicited ideas and opinions from their staff	Share responsibility for their own health and safety
Ability to seek constructive criticism from their staff; willingness to accept same	Be willing to support the boss by telling them that they are wrong!
A happiness to share the tangible (rewards) and intangible (recognition) benefits of success with their people	Take a pride in the organization and be able and willing to act as an ambassador for it
Stand up for your principles and don't get taken advantage of by your staff, or by any particular member of staff	Appreciate what they get from the organization and their manager and not take it for granted
Identify, develop and value people's potential	Work to high standards without having to be under constant supervision

→ NEXT STEPS

In this chapter we have begun to look closely at what management is, how it developed as a modern workplace discipline, and what it might mean in the context of twenty-first-century business practice. Above all, we have learned that contemporary management is about the three Cs of co-operation, compromise and consensus.

In the next few chapters, we will focus on *you*. Without a clear-headed understanding of your own goals and motivation, your 'brand' and your morale, your learning and development, and without a capacity for *self*-management, you will never be able to effectively manage others.

👍 TAKEAWAYS

What have you learned about the nature of management from this chapter? How much does this differ from your ideas before you started this workbook?

_____

_____

_____

_____

_____

_____

_____

_____

Give an example for each of the following from your own experience either as a manager or of being managed:

Co-operation

_____

_____

_____

_____

Compromise

_____

_____

_____

_____

Consensus

_____

_____

_____

_____

Given what you have read, how will you (or would you) change your management style?

_____

_____

_____

_____

_____

_____

_____

_____

_____

MANAGING YOURSELF (I): ASPIRATION AND GOAL SETTING

2

 OUTCOMES FROM THIS CHAPTER

- Understand your career aspirations.
- Assess your goal-setting management.
- Learn – or revise – common goal-setting techniques, including SMART.

Before you can effectively manage others you need to be able to manage yourself; consequently, in this and the following chapters we are going to look at how you self-manage. We will look at a number of aspects of self-management:

- where you are going, both long and short term
- what motivates you to reach your goals and how much you believe you have control over this process
- how you develop yourself
- how you keep your head when all around are losing theirs!

Your career aspirations

You are probably wondering why this chapter is about your career when the book is supposed to help you to become a better manager. There are several reasons for this. If you are not happy in your career...

- you may find it difficult to motivate yourself to achieve even your basic operational goals, never mind all the extraneous responsibilities that you have to your team as their manager
- it is very unlikely that you will be positively helpful to the careers of the people whom you manage, who may actually be very happy in theirs
- you are relatively unlikely to be happy in your life in general and this can make you into a miserable blighter. While being a 'little ray of sunshine' isn't necessarily a prerequisite for management success, it is probably fair to say that people who suck the joy out of the room are not usually very inspiring as managers and leaders.

So let us start with the big, philosophical question:

What are YOU doing on this planet?

That may be a bit too big a question to start with, so let's break it down.

COACHING SESSION 3

What are you?

Imagine that you are at a function; it could be a networking breakfast or a seminar, a cocktail party or even a big family wedding where you are meeting the family members of the other partner. Someone politely asks what you do for a living – what do you say? Try to answer the question as comprehensively as possible, without using any job titles and without naming your employer, but in fewer than 25 words.

_____

_____

_____

_____

_____

_____

_____

Take a look at your answer. Are you satisfied that you have actually summed up what you presently are/do?

Now let's look at another facet:

Why are you thus?

Many people have never really given any quality thinking time to this question, for a number of different reasons:

- For some there has never been a need because they have been predestined into a career because of their family background and parents. The most obvious examples are people like Princes William and Harry, who never got that much of a choice on the matter but were just born to it. Less obvious examples are actors such as Emilia and James Fox who clearly had a choice, but given that pretty much the whole family were thespians, ended up treading the boards themselves. For the rest of us mere mortals, if your parents ran their own business, there is clearly a strong likelihood that you will have inherited it (farming is a good example). Alternatively, if your mum or dad followed a particular profession, then there is a good chance that you 'followed in their footsteps' (doctors are quite often the children of doctors for instance).

- A similar situation to the one above is geography; if you happened to live in a location where there was one major employer, then it is relatively common that people go straight 'from the school gates to the factory gates'.

- Sometimes other significant people in your childhood may have influenced your choice of career to date – teachers, community leaders or even your friends may have 'tempted' you to follow, or avoid, certain choices.

- Many people 'fell' into a particular career simply because when they reached adulthood they needed to earn a living and so they simply took the first decent-sounding job that came along. Once in, they got stuck in a rut and have never actually moved out into anything else.

COACHING SESSION 4

Why are you this?

So, before you start any detailed soul-searching, reflect on how you came to be in the career that you are in today – was it an active choice of your own or were you fulfilling someone else's expectations and hopes? Did you choose it or did circumstances lead you to it?

1. Why do I do what I do?

_____

_____

_____

_____

_____

_____

2. When did I decide to follow this path? At what age and at what stage of my life?

_____

_____

_____

_____

_____

_____

_____

3. Who came up with the idea to enter into this career path?

_____

_____

_____

_____

_____

_____

4. What did I use to dream about being or doing when I was a child? How close is my current career to those dreams?

_____

_____

_____

_____

_____

_____

_____

_____

_____

There is no judgement attached to the answers you come up with. Many people are extremely successful, fulfilled and happy even though they never questioned their parents' chosen plans for them. Not even after a 50-year career doing something that, had they been born to a different family, they would never have pursued.

⌬⌬ COACHING SESSION 5

Why are you this?

Now that you have ascertained the truth about the past, it is time to ask yourself some more detailed questions about the present and the future. The questions are numbered 1 to 10 but they have been divided into different sections. Firstly, a question that digs out some of your core values:

1. What makes me 'proud' when I answer – *honestly* – the common conversational opening gambit of 'What do you do for a living?'?

_____

_____

_____

_____

_____

_____

_____

There is no right or wrong answer to this; neither are any answers more right or wrong – it is all about you, your situation in life, your family circumstance, your priorities and your self-esteem. The value comes in the thinking process behind coming up with an answer.

Now there is a series of questions that get you to look at what you actually do with your time. This includes how you feel about that.

2. What do I particularly like about my day-to-day work?

_____

_____

_____

_____

_____

_____

_____

3. What do I dislike about my day-to-day work?

_____

_____

_____

_____

_____

_____

_____

4. What are the highlights of the working year?

_____

_____

_____

_____

_____

_____

5. What are the low points of the working year?

_____

_____

_____

_____

_____

_____

_____

Next, let's look at how successful you are on a short-term basis.

6. What did I actually achieve today?

_____

_____

_____

_____

_____

_____

_____

_____

7. What have I achieved in the past year?

_____

_____

_____

_____

_____

_____

_____

_____

8. How happy am I with the answers I've given to questions 6 and 7?

_____

_____

_____

_____

_____

_____

_____

_____

_____

And, finally, back to the 'big picture' again:

9. Where is this job taking me?

_____

_____

_____

_____

_____

_____

10. How happy am I with the answer I've given to question 9?

_____

_____

_____

_____

_____

_____

_____

Let's take a bit of time to look at your answers to those ten questions in turn.

1 What makes me 'proud' when I answer – *honestly* – the common conversational opening gambit of 'What do you do for a living?'?

You don't have to be the CEO of a global company or the inventor of the cure for the common cold to be proud of your career. The level of pride you have is entirely self-generated and most decent human beings can be proud of just doing even a menial job well. Even if your current job is actually pretty humdrum and 'unsexy', be proud of doing it. A bit of pride does wonders for the self-esteem, and only if you have a relatively high level of self-esteem can you be a half-decent manager. If the reality is that even with a bit of thought, you can't actually have any pride in the job you do, you should be giving serious consideration to changing careers.

2 What do I particularly like about my day-to-day work?

It is a straightforward fact that, if there is little that you actually like about your day-to-day work, you are probably not a little sunbeam to be around in the workplace. That is going to make you pretty inaccessible as a manager and it will also make it rather hard for you to motivate your people. Again, if you don't like your job, you really should be thinking about changing careers. If there is lots that you like about your job, then great! You will find it easier to enthuse your staff, bosses and customers about your role and your outputs. You will be a joy to work with and consequently you will be a better manager almost by default.

3 What do I dislike about my day-to-day work?

See question 2 above. Also think about categorizing these elements into two groups:

1. things that really are an important part of my job and career

2. things that are not really important to my job and career.

Regarding the things in 1) you will just have to grit your teeth and get on with them (see below for more on the subject of motivation)

The things in 2) are tasks that you may be able to delegate appropriately and effectively (on delegation, see Chapter 9).

4 What are the highlights of the working year?

These are the times and tasks that you look forward to with happy anticipation. It is possible that there are no specific highlights of your year; that is great, so long as the reason is that you love all the year equally and every day is a great day. If, however, there are no highlights simply because every day is as grey and dull and tedious, or as hectic, pressured and stressful, as the next, then, again, you may want to look at changing careers. (Note that some people positively thrive on pressure and a hectic life. If this suits you and you are not secretly worried about 'burning out', then great! However, do ask yourself how well you manage others if you are constantly running from crisis to crisis, putting out metaphorical fires.)

5 What are the low points of the working year?

See question 4 above. Ask yourself what it is about the low points that makes them low for you. For some people, the low points are the quiet times when there is little to do and they feel unchallenged; if this is you, what can you plan to do during those low points to make them better? For some people, the low points of the year are when they have their performance appraisal with their boss; if this is you, there are two things to do.

1. Consider ways of making your performance appraisal a positive experience.

2. Consider your role as a manager carrying out performance appraisals on your staff – are *you* making it the low point of *their* year?

6 What did I actually achieve today?

Were you able to answer this with a great long list of achievements? Or did you just shrug and say 'Not a lot'? It can be very debilitating to feel as if you aren't fulfilling any purpose: you don't need necessarily to achieve something grand, or even massively noticeable to the rest of the world, but you do need to feel as if you have achieved something. Getting to the end of each and every day and wondering why you bothered is also quite disruptive to your self-esteem. In 1967 a young journalist by the name of Anthony Gray was imprisoned without trial by the communist government of China. He was held in solitary confinement for over two years in an eight-foot-by-eight-foot room. He had no idea when (or even if) he would be released. Part of the reason that he managed to stay sane was that he set himself a plan for each month and he then kept a detailed diary of his achievements. Many of these achievements were very small and apparently had little bearing on the big scheme of things; he wasn't digging a tunnel or building an aeroplane, after all. They were little things such as to trying to get hold of a book to read, to write a letter, or to do his exercises. Just by keeping his focus on what he had achieved each day, week and month, he helped to keep his sanity and to keep up his morale.

7 What have I achieved in the past year?

'Rome wasn't built in a day,' as they say. Sometimes it is easier to see your achievements over a longer period than a day.

8 How happy am I with the answers I've given to questions 6 and 7.

This is, of course, entirely a subjective question. You may have achieved nothing at all over the course of your entire career to date, but you may be entirely happy about that. It may be that, frankly, you just don't really care whether you achieve anything. However, if that is the case, you are unlikely to be reading this book! It may also be that your career is simply what puts a roof over your head and food in your belly, and that you get your *raison d'être* from other activities in life, such as your family, church or football team. If that is the case, you have to ask yourself whether you would be better off trying to be a manager somewhere closer to your heart.

9 Where is this job taking me?

You need to consider this question in the long, medium and short terms. In the long term, is the job you are doing actually appropriate for where you really want to spend the rest of your life? How good a foundation is it for you to base your 'three score years and ten'? Is it leading you to an acceptable position where you can start and bring up a family (if that is your medium-term aim in life)? How is it affecting you on a short-term basis: are you grumpy at the end of each day/week/month? Are you too tired/bored/depressed to enjoy being alive?

10 How happy am I with the answer I've given to question 9?

Again, the 'happiness' element is subjective: you may be genuinely happy being utterly exhausted by 6 o'clock every evening, and, if you are, then great. That means that your job is incredibly fulfilling, whether it is saving lives or digging ditches. But if you really would like the energy to do something active at the weekend, you may need to start questioning your current job. You may be happy that your job is fun and challenging, even though you accept that it isn't taking you anywhere. You may be happy that your job is great today. Even if you know that it isn't sustainable, and you cannot possibly still be doing it in 15 years' time, you may be very happy with your job now. But consider how happy you will be as you reach the point where you cannot continue and have to change: what effect will that have on your ability as a manager then?

What we have been trying to do so far is assess the foundation for your management style. A manager can really only be effective when he/she is happy and committed to their role. If you can't see the point, and you can't muster any enthusiasm, then you will find it almost impossible to motivate others to follow you. Even the best manager can turn into a liability if he/she loses their inner purpose, but people with a passion and a mission tend naturally to become leaders … simply because other people can see the passion and the mission and follow.

This section has asked you to look at your longer-term career motivation. Getting that right (for you) is a great foundation upon which to build your management style and success. You also have to look at your shorter-term motivation: your daily, weekly and monthly goals and targets. That is where the next section of the book is going to take you.

MANAGING YOUR SHORT-TERM GOALS

In this section, we are going to look at your management of your own short-term goals. In Chapter 11 we will look at setting and agreeing goals for your team and your individual team members, but for now we are concentrating on you.

Before we get too far into the topic, let's get some nomenclature sorted out. We are not drawing any differentiation between goals, targets or objectives. We are also mixing in the goals, targets or objectives that may be formally yours at work, and the ones you may informally 'set' in your private life and or career.

⚌⚌ COACHING SESSION 6

Diagnostic test: your short-terms goals

Carry out this short diagnostic test to assess your personal current situation.

What I* am going** to achieve*** this week	
Operationally (This could include personal sales work, problem solving, dealing with customer issues, planning for the next quarter, etc.)	1. 2. 3.
In terms of managing my team (This could include dealing with good and poor performance, setting objectives for individuals, carrying out appraisals, coaching, communicating with the team, etc.)	1. 2. 3.
In terms of managing for my team (This could include promoting the team to senior managers/other departments, recruiting a new person, etc.)	1. 2. 3

* Note that the word is 'I', not 'we' ... the buck stops here! If you have difficulty in completing this diagnostic, it suggests that you haven't got a good grip on your short-term goals.

** Note that the verb is 'going to', not 'trying to', or 'aiming to' ... this is definite!

*** Note that this is what will be 'achieved', not 'done'.

What I am going to achieve this month.	
Operationally (This could include personal sales work, problem solving, dealing with customer issues, planning for the next quarter, etc.)	1. 2. 3.
In terms of managing my team (this could include dealing with good and poor performance, setting objectives for individuals, carrying out appraisals, coaching, communicating with the team, etc.)	1. 2. 3.
In terms of managing for my team (This could include promoting the team to senior managers/other departments, recruiting a new person, etc.)	1. 2. 3.

Q. So what?

A. If a journey of a thousand miles starts with a single step, and the first steps don't get taken, the journey will never be completed. Or if the early steps get taken in a random direction, imagine how far off course you might be when you finally clock up your thousand miles!

If you found it quite easy to complete the diagnostic, ask yourself two questions:

1. 'Were the answers already in my head, consciously?' In other words, 'How likely is it that I would have actually achieved all of those things if I hadn't been prompted by the diagnostic?'

2. 'Am I actually happy that the answers I have given represent an adequate level of achievement and challenge for me?' If not, then look to beef up your aspirations; if they do, then great.

You may well have been trained in the setting of goals, targets and objectives already, so if the following is revision, please bear with it and read it anyway – revision is usually useful! Here are some proven goal-setting 'models':

SMART

Possibly the single most common goal-setting model in the world today, SMART is used by most organizations at some point. It is a simple acronym for the five-point 'critical' features of an effective goal.

S Specific

A goal has to be specific in terms of the characteristics of achievement. This is not the same as the characteristics of input/effort/activity/trying.

For instance:

Characteristics of input/effort/activity/trying	Characteristics of achievement
Phone 50 prospects off the target list	Book three new sales meetings
Spend two hours practising my touch-typing	Reach a point where I can consistently touch-type 20 words a minute with correct keystrokes
Mop the floor	Get the floor clean
Meet with the client	Get a detailed brief from the client so we can formulate a meaningful price quote.

Many managers find it quite difficult to actually nail down the specifics of the goals they set for themselves and their people. The reason is usually that we draw goals and objectives from job descriptions and job descriptions tend to describe actions and activities. Actions tend to be verbs and verbs are often not conducive to coming to a conclusion. For example, if we set a goal 'to liaise with the IT department', how do we know when we have liaised enough?

A simple methodology to use when you are struggling is to ask 'Why?' For instance:

To liaise with the IT department.

Why?

So they understand our requirements for the new software.

Now we are being more specific and could therefore set the objective as:

To provide the IT department with a detailed specification of what we need the new software to do.

Obviously, this then leads you to some sub-objectives, such as working out for yourselves what you need the new software to do, before you liaise with the IT department. So, by setting a specific objective, you often find that you prevent yourself from ending up wasting time (and damaging your credibility).

> ### Scene: the meeting with the IT department
>
> **IT Manager:** So Chris, you've called this meeting to tell us what you need us to create for you by way of new software…
>
> **You:** Yes, the old software just doesn't perform with the recent changes in the product and logistics since the merger.
>
> **IT Manager:** OK, so what particular functionality do you need?
>
> **You:** Well, we need it to be better.
>
> **IT Manager:** Oooookaaaay, er, how many users will need passwords and access?
>
> **You:** Good question. I'll have to ask the rest of the team how many of them use it.
>
> **IT Manager:** OK, and how many products do you need the software to categorize?
>
> **You:** Um, I think at last count there were over 4,500.
>
> **IT Manager:** And is that growing?
>
> **You:** I'm not sure I'll have to speak to my boss.
>
> **IT Manager:** OK, and how many customer files will you need?
>
> **You:** Er, I'll need to speak to sales about that…

(You get the gist here … without setting yourself a meaningfully specific goal, you end up with a load of tasks to complete and a reputation for being clueless!)

M Measurable

This is often inextricably linked with the specific element but the real test is to ask 'How could someone else actually tell whether I have achieved that goal or not?' Professor Richard Wiseman, of the University of Hertfordshire, carried out a study in 2007 of over 3,000 people (in the UK and US) and their goal-setting achievement of success. He found that there was a 22-per-cent increase in success (especially noticeable in men) when the goal was immediately measurable.

Measurable can be a definite Yes/No answer or a proportionate answer. For example, let's say you have a goal to complete all (100 per cent) your team's annual appraisal paperwork and carry out all the one-to-one meetings. In reality, you have completed all the paperwork and you have had the one to ones with 7 of your 11 team members.

You can be said to have failed in your goal.

You can also be said to have achieved 63 per cent of it.

Another form of measurability could be something relative: for example, 'I'm going to make more sales than you.' In this instance, although the measurement is movable, it still has a definable quality.

A Achievable

There is no point in setting an objective that you either know you cannot achieve or that you don't believe is achievable.

The former is usually simply because the actual achievement is outside your sphere of control: you can try to save the whale, and you can influence others to try to save the whale, but you can't actually guarantee that the whale is, in fact, saveable.

Similarly, in the former case, if you don't believe that the goal can be achieved, then you are probably simply going through the motions when you set it as a goal and start to attempt it. If the goal in question is self-motivated, then you need to question why you actually set it: who were you trying to kid? If the goal in question is a goal 'imposed' on you by your boss/organization, then you really need to question why you accepted it: have you set yourself up to fail?

COACHING SESSION 7

Setting yourself up to fail by accepting unachievable goals

Below are eight scenarios that are often given as reasons (or excuses) for failing to achieve goals:

1. Because it is an area of my job description that I don't actually like/agree with or excel at. (For example, selling insurance is part of the job description of most bank managers, but many bank managers don't like being thought of as life insurance salespeople.)

2. Because somebody up high came up with a big target, and this is my (unreasonable) proportion. I don't think the number is actually attainable, but it wasn't negotiable.

3. I'm supposed to display a 'can-do' attitude and so I accepted a goal that I didn't think was achievable rather than appear negative.

4. It isn't my place to argue with the boss.

5. The current economic conditions suggest that, if I hadn't agreed, I may have been out of work by now.

6. The goal looked achievable at the time that I agreed it, but now the external factors have changed and it has become impossible. (For example, I agreed to handle all enquiries and respond with an answer within 24 hours, but the number of enquiries has quadrupled and I simply cannot cope.)

7. The goal looked achievable at the time that I agreed it, but now the internal factors have changed and it is now impossible. (For example, when I agreed it, it was one of only two targets I was going to achieve, but since the reorganization I now have seven different targets and there simply isn't time to devote to them all.)

8. The goal looked achievable at the time that I agreed it, but with hindsight, I agreed it in ignorance of several factors (that were in existence at the time) but about which I was then unaware. I have since discovered this, but now I will have to admit my failings if I try to get the goal 'downgraded'.

Ask yourself three questions with regard to each of the eight scenarios:

To what extent have I found myself in these situations in the past?

1 _____

2 _____

3 _____

4 _____

5 _____

6 _____

7 _____

8 _____

How will I avoid getting into these situations in the future?

1
_____

_____

2
_____

_____

3
_____

_____

4
_____

_____

5
_____

_____

6
_____

_____

7
_____

_____

8
_____

_____

What will I do to extricate myself from these situations (if I realize that I am already in them or if I were to discover this in the future)?

1

_____

_____

_____

2

_____

_____

_____

3

_____

_____

_____

4

_____

_____

_____

5

_____

_____

_____

6

_____

_____

_____

7

_____

_____

_____

8

_____

_____

_____

R Relevant

'Relevant' in this instance means that achievement of this goal actively contributes to the big picture. For instance, if you are a sales manager, all your short- and medium-term workplace goals should be directly relevant to increasing or maintaining sales revenue. Obviously, if you are a sales manager now, but you hanker after a career in show business, you may have some short- to medium-term non-workplace goals that relate to your intended career. The relevance of goals is very important when a person is suffering from 'goal-diffusion', but we'll come onto that later in this section.

T Time-bound

There are two elements to this:

1 Actually having a **deadline** to achieve a goal by. This should be specific rather than either generic (*generic* means 'as soon as possible' or 'as soon as viable' or 'when I get around to it') or ambiguous (i.e. by the end of the week – is that 5 p.m., midnight on Friday, midnight on Sunday?)

Without any deadline, the likelihood is that it will simply never get done.

2 Actually having some sort of 'enforcement' on the deadline set.

> *'I love deadlines. I like the whooshing sound they make as they fly by.'*
>
> Douglas Adams, writer

The most ineffectual manager 'sets' deadlines and then signally fails to make sure that they are actually met. This is just as relevant for one's own individual goals as for the goals you set for your staff. Allowing yourself an excuse whenever you fail to achieve simply negates the whole point of striving to achieve in the first place.

Failure + Excuse/Reason ≠ Achievement

Professor Richard Wiseman's studies also showed a 10-per-cent improved likelihood of success (especially for women) when they had made a point of telling others about their self-generated goal. It is reasonable to presume that the potential loss of face in failing was a form of 'enforcement'.

OTHER GOAL-SETTING TECHNIQUES

SMART is probably the most commonly used model, but others exist, for instance:

SHABBY

- **S Subject** This gives some context for the goal in question, for example, it may be 'Team Development' if it is a goal relating to your completion of your team's annual appraisals.
- **H Headline** Rather like a newspaper headline or a blog article title this aims to sum up the goal in a single sentence. Usually you will fit the time element into the headline.

- **Ⓐ Actions**   The Actions are the detailed practical steps that you will put in place to ensure you reach the goal. (As you can imagine this can become more of a planning activity than simply goal setting – this can be helpful to assist in checking the achievability of the goal.)

- **ⒷⒷ Bonus or Benefit**   This provides the rationale for achieving the goal. This can therefore be the business benefit, if the goal is a purely work related one, or it could be the personal payoff if the goal is a private one. The intention here is to support the motivation for you to achieve the goal.

- **Ⓨ Yes?**   This is your final sign off to say that you commit to the goal: that is, you believe it can be done and will do it.

PRISM

The PRISM model covers all five points of the SMART mnemonic and adds two more. PRISM is an acronym for Personal, Realistic, Interesting, Specific and Measurable.

Ⓟ Personal   This means personal accountability as well as unique.

Ⓡ Realistic   This is similar to 'Achievable' in SMART and also includes the time bound element.

Ⓘ Interesting   Because people put more effort into something that is of interest to them, this could be because of the personal preference of the individual, the benefit to them as a person in their career or the business benefit of the task.

Ⓢ Specific   The detail of the required outcome, as in SMART.

Ⓜ Measurable   Again, as in SMART.

With all three of the above models it is worth remembering that each goal doesn't have to have the requisite 5 (SMART & PRISM) or 6 (SHABBY) separate sentences: it can be summed up in one sentence with the requisite points all covered ... for example:

I'm going to lose two stone in weight by my next pre-surgery review on the 9th of April.

HOW MANY GOALS SHOULD I HAVE AT ANY ONE TIME?

There is no definitive answer to this question: different people, at different times will have different answers. If your life is in turmoil, for instance, because of ill health, then just two or three goals can be too many to cope with. Conversely, having nothing (or very little) to strive for can be similarly debilitating. Having goals can give meaning to life, whereas trying to achieve too much at once can cause rapid burnout.

The issue is not solely about the number of differing goals but also the magnitude of the individual goals and the sum thereof:

1. Negotiating peace between two warring nations is a single massive goal, whereas negotiating the price of a new house is a relatively medium-sized goal, whereas negotiating with your three-year-old over bedtime is a relatively small goal (although at the time it can seem more difficult to actually achieve than world peace!).

2. Saving the planet is a huge goal, whereas saving £10,000 is (for most of us) a fairly large goal, while saving five minutes a day on the walk to work by walking a bit faster is a relatively small goal.

🗩🗩 COACHING SESSION 8

Your optimum level of goal setting

To find your 'optimum normal level', take the time to complete the table below.

When I was at my most productive (describe the period):*	What I was striving to achieve at this time (quite probably not formalized goals…):	What I did achieve:
	1	1
	2	2
	3	3
	4	4
	5	5
When I was at my least productive (describe the period):	What I was striving to achieve at this time (quite probably not formalized goals…):	What I did achieve:
	1	1
	2	2
	3	3
	4	4
	5	5

What does this experience tell me about the number and magnitude of goals that suits me?	How few goals do I need to keep me productive?	How many differing goals will start to cause me to lose focus?

* Try to think of this not just in relation to having your nose to the grindstone and flogging yourself to death, but when you where highly productive and had high morale with it.

The exercise above should help you to find your optimum level of goals and objectives. This is critically important because it affects your ability and motivation to achieve. People with too many goals tend to get 'goal diffusion': they are trying to achieve so many different things that they lose sight of priorities and end up failing to achieve several of them. Concentrating on the important things helps you to achieve them and also helps to keep you motivated.

 NEXT STEPS

In this chapter I have turned the spotlight on you. I have asked you to look as honestly as you can at your own career aspirations and to assess your own goal-setting capacity. You may have found this difficult, even painful, but the goal was to get you to think about how well you manage yourself. You may not have liked what you discovered about yourself, but at least you are in a much stronger position to take your management skills forward.

In the next chapter, the spotlight is still on you, and this time it is your motivation that we will be looking at, as well as at how you 'lead' yourself.

👍 **TAKEAWAYS**

What have you learned about your career aspirations from this chapter?

_____

_____

_____

_____

_____

_____

_____

_____

_____

_____

What have you learned about your goal setting from this chapter?

_____

_____

_____

_____

_____

_____

_____

_____

_____

_____

_____

Given what you have read in this chapter, how will you (or would you) change your management style?

_____

_____

_____

_____

_____

_____

_____

_____

_____

_____

_____

_____

_____

MANAGING YOURSELF (II): MOTIVATION

3

 OUTCOMES FROM THIS CHAPTER

- Understand how to manage your motivation.
- Learn about the nature of proactivity and why it is so important.

Motivation is a fascinating subject: if you can find a way to motivate yourself to do certain things, then life becomes so much better than if you just 'go with the flow'. The important element is to motivate yourself to do 'certain' things rather than other things ... or nothing!

An interesting way of looking at this is to ask yourself what people mean when they describe someone (or themselves) as 'demotivated':

- Do they really mean that they have no motivation whatsoever? That, apart from the unconscious actions of breathing and a heartbeat, they genuinely can't summon the enthusiasm to do anything else?

- Or do they mean that there is actually something else they would rather be doing? In other words, something that motivates them more, that is higher up their list of priorities? Even if that something is actually just sleeping or vegetating in front of a computer game or a TV screen.

We will return to this particular issue later in Chapter 13 when we look at your role as a manager in motivating other people. In this section we are looking at what motivates *you*: once you understand your own motivations, you will find it easier to motivate others.

THE HIERARCHY OF NEEDS

What are the things that motivate you? What things make your job worth doing and make you want to get up in the morning and go to work? What are the things that you want to do at the weekend that you daydream about and plan during the quiet moments of the working week? It isn't just the concept of a pay cheque at the end of the month (not that that isn't important), but there are other things that either you do, or other people do for you or to you, that motivate you.

Some of the things that motivate you will be the things that psychologists and management thinkers such as Abraham Maslow have talked about in his 'Hierarchy of Needs'. Maslow stated that we all need:

- **Shelter, food and water** – that is what the salary is for!

- **Security and safety** – that is what all the health and safety rules and employment law is for; it is also what the 'psychological contract' is all about: that sense of trust between the people who work for the organization and the people who make the big decisions. Outside work, it is what society's laws and norms of behaviour provide.

- **A sense of belonging to a team, tribe, gang or family** – that is part of what the organizational 'brand' is about... It is one of the reasons that your employer (probably) has their name over the door or why you have a business card or company work wear. It is the source of family pride and nationalism.

- **Status, responsibility, a sense of worth** – if you aren't a manager, then some of the previous paragraph still applies, it is also what a lot of employers' Corporate Social Responsibility (CSR) programmes are all about. It is also what the management perks are for: the salary, the bigger or better car/office and the job title ... things that make you look good to other people who aren't in your 'gang'.

- **Self-actualization** – this is the final level where people need to do things just because they can and it makes them feel good.

But there is more than that even. These things you'd be looking for wherever you existed, whomever you worked for, and whatever country you lived in. So what are the day-to-day things that actually make you work that bit harder, or smarter?

◯◯ COACHING SESSION 9

My motivation: self-assessment

Answer the following questions for yourself. Be honest, but think about the answers quite deeply.

1. Why do I work in the trade or profession that I follow?
2. Why do I work for my current employer?
3. What makes me happy when I wake up in the morning during the working week?
4. What makes me satisfied at the end of the day during the working week?
5. How much do I miss the atmosphere of my workplace when I'm on holiday?

(There aren't any answer lines for you to record answers to these questions because they are very similar to the questions in Coaching session 5, so look back at the answers you gave there and revisit them in the light of the actual wording of these questions.)

These questions are all related to *subjective* things such as happiness and feelings, but that is what motivation is all about. Motivation isn't just about money: so long as a person has enough money to live on, then motivation is effected by a whole range of other factors. Later in this book (in Chapter 13) we will look the effect you can have on the motivation of the people you manage; at that point, we will look at the full range.

PROACTIVITY

Back in the 1980s, Dr Stephen R Covey was motivated to write a book entitled *Seven Habits of Highly Effective People*. It became a bestseller and has now sold over 25 million copies and is translated into pretty much every language on the planet. One of the 'habits' he identified was 'proactivity'. The word has now become commonplace, but at the outset it was a newish word and quite a new concept. Covey was talking about the mental condition that rejected being 'deterministic' about what happened to you and went on around you. 'Proactivity' encourages you to get off your butt and take control of things. He was talking about making your own decisions – 'paddling your own canoe', as it were.

In 2012 Justin Menkes wrote a book called *Better under Pressure*. This book is a distillation of the attitudes and actions of business leaders who have succeeded, not only when times were OK, but especially when things were going pear-shaped for their organizations. His term for Covey's 'proactivity' is a 'sense of agency'.

In both cases the premise is that you can take one of two views:

1. You just sit back and take the view that 'life is hard', and that there is nothing, or very little, that you can do to change or control the situation in order to improve your lot (and the lot of the people for whom you are responsible)'

   or

2. You can make an effort to change things for the better.

COACHING SESSION 10

Proactivity: self-assessment

Consider the following situations for you as a manager and the multiple-choice options listed below each one. Remember, we are looking here not at 'problem solving' in itself, but at your willingness to demonstrate proactivity or show a 'sense of agency'.

1. You have recently been appointed to be the team leader of a team that you haven't worked with before. You have a brief handover from the outgoing team leader who tells you that one particular team member – we'll call her Joan – always comes in about half an hour late each day. 'But that is just the way she is' is the rationalization he gives you. Once you are established as the team leader, do you:

a. Discipline Joan for lateness.

b. Take Joan aside and tell her that from now on she must come to work on time according to contract, because otherwise she is technically breaking the rules.

c. Simply allow the status quo to continue on the grounds that custom and practice now dictate that it is too late to change things or that you don't want to alienate yourself so early.

d. Rewrite everyone's contract to a new set of working hours to prove that you are now in charge and that a 'new broom sweeps clean'.

2. You are leading your team and your manager has one of her regular 'press the flesh and show the flag' meetings with one of your clients. At the meeting, the client cheekily asks for something pretty outrageous in terms of extra service and your boss agrees unconditionally. Your boss has told you about the new agreement and you can see that this is going to mean that people will have to work much longer (and antisocial) hours. Do you:

a. Shrug your shoulders, rationalize the fact that it is a done deal and just bear the extra burden, spreading it equally around the team with a grumble about the management.

b. Stoically accept the new situation and force the team to shoulder the burden, but don't take on extra hours yourself on the grounds that 'rank has its privileges'.

c. Arrange a private meeting with the manager concerned and explain the challenges that her actions have created; then offer whatever help you can to assist her in making whatever staffing changes are needed to return people to reasonable working hours while not upsetting the client.

d. Arrange a private meeting with the manager concerned: explain the challenges that her actions have created, then ask her to go back to the client and either return to the original service agreement or charge extra to cover the extra cost of delivery.

e. Go to the client direct, explain that your manager was out of order agreeing to changes in the service agreement, explain the problems that this has caused for the team and ask politely to return to the previous agreement.

f. Go to your manager's manager and lodge a complaint that your manager's actions were inappropriate and that you would like her to be reprimanded.

While the larger element of value you can obtain from this coaching session is simply your own considerations of the multiple choice answers, let us look briefly at what each might mean about your level of determinism vs. proactivity or your sense of agency.

Question 1

a. *Discipline Joan for lateness.*

While this shows a strong sense of agency, it may be a little drastic at this stage. See Chapter 11, on 'Managing your team members' performance'.

b. *Take Joan aside and tell her that from now on she must come to work on time according to contract, because otherwise she is technically breaking the rules.*

This shows a strong sense of agency coupled with a proportionate actual response.

c. *Simply allow the status quo to continue on the grounds that custom and practice now dictate that it is too late to change things or that you don't want to alienate yourself so early.*

This shows a complete lack of a sense of agency and a high degree of determinism. It will come back to bite you in the long run.

d. *Rewrite everyone's contract to a new set of working hours to prove that you are now in charge and a 'new broom sweeps clean'.*

While this shows a sense of agency, it is again probably disproportionate to the matter in hand. It is also suggestive of change for its own sake or even collective punishment, neither of which is generally a good idea.

Question 2

a. *Shrug your shoulders, rationalize the fact that it is a done deal and just bear the extra burden, spreading it equally around the team with a grumble about the management.*

This would show no sense of agency at all, except the grumbling. Even that is debateable: grumbling to someone about something that is outside their control is not demonstrating a sense of agency or proactivity.

b. *Stoically accept the new situation and force the team to shoulder the burden, but don't take on extra hours yourself the grounds that 'rank has its privileges'.*

Again, this is not demonstrating a proactive approach. While it can be interpreted as a 'can do' attitude towards the boss's directive, it is completely determined by the boss, who may be genuinely ignorant of the consequences of her actions. Personally escaping the implications of the change may seem like a proactive action but is more likely to be interpreted by all and sundry as selfish. Proactivity and a sense of agency are self-motivations, and are properly 'egocentric', but are not selfish acts at the cost of others.

c. *Arrange a private meeting with the manager concerned and explain the challenges that her actions have created; then offer whatever help you can to assist her in making whatever staffing changes are needed to return people to reasonable working hours while not upsetting the client.*

This is a properly proactive approach: not only are you bringing the matter to your manager's attention for action, but also offering to assist, as is proper, since the client is one that you already serve.

d. *Arrange a private meeting with the manager concerned: explain the challenges that her actions have created, then ask her to go back to the client and either return to the original service agreement or charge extra to cover the extra cost of delivery.*

This is also a properly proactive approach. You have brought the matter to the boss's attention for her action and clearly set out your needs in the situation, but then left her to do her job. Proactivity and a sense of agency are not the same as taking responsibility from other people: just taking your own responsibility.

e. *Go to the client direct, explain that your manager was out of order agreeing to changes in the service agreement, explain the problems that this has caused for the team and ask politely to return to the previous agreement.*

Again, while this may be seen as a 'can do' approach it is also shouldering someone else's burden, which is not proactivity. It can also be seen as disloyal and undermining the boss in the eyes of the client, which rather looks as if you are going native... Your client won't be the one writing your appraisal or deciding whether to declare you redundant; your boss will.

f. *Go to your manager's manager and lodge a complaint that your manager's actions where inappropriate and that you would like her to be reprimanded.*

Although this course of action is more proactive than a) and b) above (in so far as you are doing something rather than nothing), it is probably disproportionate. It is also likely to have longer-term negative consequences, for you and your boss.

So how did you fare? Did you have a sense of agency? Are you proactive? To be an effective manager and to be better under pressure you need to be...

'LEADING' YOURSELF

Another way of looking at the matter of proactivity is to consider it as a matter of self-leadership. In many situations, a 'leader' is appointed, and therefore leadership is a position, a title or a formal role.

A leader isn't a leader until or unless he/she has some followers. There are two types of follower:

- those who follow willingly and fully and will continue to follow even when the leader isn't watching

- those who the leader has to 'drag' – that is, those who have been given the job role of 'followers' but in their heart of hearts they aren't really that interested. These folk may 'follow' because:

  - it is the line of least resistance

  - no other leader would have them

  - they are scared of the consequences of not following

  - they may follow out of sheer habit.

In many situations, there may actually be no particular person who is the formal, appointed or elected leader – for example, in a relationship, a band, among a group of friends on a night out or on a holiday together, or among a group of peers ... or even when you are alone. In these circumstances, leadership isn't a formal job title; it is a state of mind.

In these situations, 'leadership' is reliant upon one particular aspect of a person's mentality: do I have the right to exert any level of control over the matter in hand? As there is no formal authority you may have no direct control over the outcome, but you do have direct control over your actions; this may have a degree of influence over the outcome.

Think of it as a sliding scale:

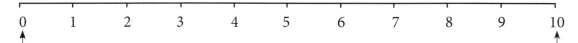

| 0 | 1 | 2 | 3 | 4 | 5 | 6 | 7 | 8 | 9 | 10 |

At the 0 end you have no control at all over the matter; only control over your own actions (even if that control is a conscious and deliberate decision to do nothing). Your actions may have some influence over the situation or over other people's actions.

At the 10 end you have complete control over the outcome of the matter as a whole, as well as your own actions.

🗩🗩 COACHING SESSION 11

Self-leadership: self-assessment

Consider the following questions and the multiple-choice options below each:

1. You become aware that one of your peers is stealing from the organization. This is on a pretty minor scale: pinching stationary supplies, using the office phone for long personal calls, surfing the Internet for an hour a day doing home shopping and booking their holiday. The person concerned makes little attempt to hide it except from the boss. Which of the following do you do?

   a. Privately discuss it with them, explaining that it all adds up to a significant amount and it also sets a bad example to his staff.
   b. Just ignore it; after all, it isn't your job to manage him, besides which you have no authority to do anything.
   c. Just ignore it on the grounds that there is no victim in this 'crime'.
   d. Recognize that he is getting away with it and that it is the equivalent of him being paid more than you, so you might as well copy the behaviour, and so start doing it yourself.
   e. Go and see your boss (or your peer's boss) and report him as a thief.

f. Send an anonymous report to the boss or HR to report him either personally or stating that someone ('who shall remain nameless') is stealing.

2. You started your current job nine months ago after a brief period of unemployment following redundancy from another employer. Your current role is a complete change from your previous career and is less senior than the position you lost. This morning, on your way to work, you saw a job advertisement for exactly the role that you used to have just before you were made redundant… but it is with your current employer. It pays marginally more than you used to earn and a lot more than you are earning presently. Do you:

   a. Immediately contact the relevant person, explain your credentials and ask to be fast-tracked through the selection process
   b. Apply as per the instructions in the advertisement and take your chances with all the outside candidates
   c. Presume that, since your employer is aware of your previous career and has not already offered you the role, you have already been considered and rejected, and therefore do nothing
   d. Assume the situation in c) but complain to your peers and family that the management is too stupid to recognize the talent within its own ranks

Again let's look at the level of self-leadership you are demonstrating in these circumstances:

Question 1

a. *Privately discuss it with them, explaining that it all adds up to a significant amount and it also sets a bad example to his staff.*

This is a properly proportionate proactive demonstration of a sense of agency.

b. *Just ignore it; after all, it isn't your job to manage him, besides which you have no authority to do anything.*

This is a complete demonstration of a complete lack of proactivity (it is also, sadly, the most common reaction to the situation!)

c. *Just ignore it on the grounds that there is no victim in this 'crime'.*

Again, this is a complete whitewash, but using a different justification. One element about proactivity or having a sense of agency is the way we often rationalize our actions (or lack of action). The very fact that we come up with 'excuses' suggests that in our heart of hearts we know that we should stand up and do something: 'For evil to triumph, it is only necessary that good men do nothing'.

d. *Recognize that he is getting away with it and that it is the equivalent of him being paid more than you so you might as well copy the behaviour, and so start doing it yourself.*

Again, some people think that stealing is a proactive activity, on the grounds that it is doing something rather than nothing. Bearing in mind that Covey

MANAGING YOURSELF (II): MOTIVATION

was a preacher (as well as a university lecturer), I think we can presume that he wouldn't agree! Generally, this response also damages the overall motivational element of a sense of belonging... unless it is motivating to you to belong to the criminal fraternity!

e. *Go and see your boss (or your peer's boss) and report him as a thief.*

This is a proactive approach in so far as it is action that is morally correct. Depending on the circumstances, it may also be the most politically acceptable approach, although it is one that will clearly have irreversible implications and consequences, when you have to give evidence.

f. *Send an anonymous report to the boss or HR to report him either personally or stating that someone ('who shall remain nameless') is stealing.*

This is a proactive approach in so far as it is action that is morally correct. Depending on the circsumstances it may be the best approach.

Question 2

a. *Immediately contact the relevant person, explain your credentials and ask to be fast-tracked through the selection process.*

This is a properly proactive response. It is not selfish to ask to be fast-tracked in this instance: you already work for the organization, so they have no real need to take up character references, and you are already inducted, so your training/settling in period would be quicker and cheaper for them. Also, there is significantly less danger of you not fitting culturally into the organization.

b. *Apply as per the instructions in the advertisement and take your chances with all the outside candidates.*

This may be fully proactive *if* the organization insists (for reasons of compliance with equality and diversity policies) that they won't fast-track you.

c. *Presume that, since your employer is aware of your previous career and has not already offered you the role, you have already been considered and rejected and therefore do nothing.*

This is, again, a cop-out!

d. *Assume the situation in c) but complain to your peers and family that the management is too stupid to recognize the talent within its own ranks.*

Again, this is not proactive. Complaining to people who are powerless is not a substitute for sensible action; it is just whingeing. It may make you feel better in the short term but it achieves nothing above and beyond that.

How did you fare in these situations; how much proactivity did you demonstrate?

NEXT STEPS

As a manager, you have to be, and remain, motivated to do the things that your job, employer, position and staff need you to do. As a person seeking to succeed in life (not necessarily or just in a corporate career), you need to be motivated to do something and to do the right thing.

If you can't or won't or don't do this, your 'brand image' with people will be affected. You will be seen by people as a lesser character and they will be less likely to actually choose to follow you – so you won't be their real leader, regardless of what your business card may say. It is on the importance of your 'personal brand' and how you can develop that brand that we will focus next.

TAKEAWAYS

What have you learned about your motivation from this chapter?

_____

_____

_____

_____

_____

_____

_____

_____

_____

_____

_____

What have you learned about your level of proactivity from this chapter?

_____

_____

_____

_____

_____

_____

_____

_____

_____

_____

_____

Write down your thoughts about why self-motivation and proactivity are such key 'virtues' in an excellent manager.

_____

_____

_____

_____

_____

_____

_____

_____

_____

_____

MANAGING YOURSELF (III): YOUR 'PERSONAL BRAND' AND HOW TO DEVELOP IT

4

 OUTCOMES FROM THIS CHAPTER

- Understand the importance of your brand image.
- Learn how to develop your brand effectively.

Everyone has a personal brand image. Your brand image is what other people think of you, and in this shallow era of social media your brand image is very important to your effectiveness, both as a member of society and as a manager.

There are two elements to consider here:

1. your brand expectation
2. your brand experience.

Let's look at each of these in turn.

YOUR BRAND EXPECTATION

This is the image that you want people to have of you. Imagine the following situation:

A member of your team gets into a lift/elevator with another person from the organization and that person has just been seconded to work for you on a project for six months. The other person mentions this to your team member and asks him or her to answer the following question....

'What is [your name] like to work for?'

What would you hope the team member would say? (Note that the question is 'hope'; ignore matters of confidentiality, loyalty, discretion and so on... Concentrate on what you hope the reality might be for the person who has worked for you for some time.)

Here is a list of characteristics to help you to think about this:

- approachable
- charitable
- considerate
- dedicated
- determined
- energetic
- exciting
- fair

- focused
- fun
- helpful
- honest
- inspiring
- intuitive
- knowledgeable
- meticulous

- motivational
- organized
- proactive
- reliable
- supportive
- thoughtful
- trustworthy
- visionary

🗨 COACHING SESSION 12

Your brand image

See whether you can write the 'hoped for' thumbnail description in no more than 50 words.

_____

_____

_____

_____

_____

_____

_____

_____

So much for the brand image that you hope for... Now let's look at the brand experience.

YOUR BRAND EXPERIENCE

The brand experience is the reality for the person who has it. Where the expectation above is about what you hope people think of you, your brand experience is what they *actually* think of you, based on the way you have treated them and behaved towards them in the past.

What this means, of course, is that not everyone will have the same brand experience of you, for example:

Chris is a member of your team whom you inherited from your predecessor. Chris is a bit lazy and slipshod, doing the bare minimum to keep out of trouble but never making much effort. Chris was allowed to get away with this under your predecessor. You are determined to get Chris to improve and so have weekly reviews where you discuss goals, motivation, actions and results. These meetings are always like pulling teeth since Chris clearly resents your interference with an otherwise carefree life. You also frequently catch Chris coasting at work and you 'manage' this each and every time it happens.

Pat is one of your best team members. Pat clearly loves a challenge and, with your support, always rises to it. You have a monthly review with Pat which is quick and easy due to Pat's high motivation. You frequently 'catch' Pat doing a great job and take each opportunity to offer some appreciation and recognition of Pat's dedication and success.

- Chris's brand experience of you is that you are a 'pain in the backside' taskmaster who just won't let up.
- Pat's brand experience of you is that you are a great manager who motivates and supports his/her staff.

If we consider that list of hoped for characteristics, we can now look at some potential alternatives to the 'nice' things we would have hoped to hear if we had been a fly-on-the-wall in that lift!

- approachable or aloof
- charitable or mean
- considerate or heartless
- dedicated or haphazard (or dedicated to the 'wrong' things)
- determined or submissive
- energetic or sluggish
- exciting or dull
- fair or biased
- focused or all-over-the-place
- fun or depressing
- helpful or dismissive
- honest or shifty
- inspiring or draining
- intuitive or thick-skinned
- knowledgeable or clueless
- meticulous or lackadaisical
- motivational or destructive
- organized or chaotic
- proactive or laissez-faire
- reliable or inconsistent
- supportive or uncaring
- thoughtful or impulsive
- trustworthy or unreliable
- visionary or lost

⚏ COACHING SESSION 13

Your brand experience

Now let's rerun that imagined situation:

A member of your team gets into a lift with another person from the organization and that person has just been seconded to work for you on a project for six months. The other person mentions this to your team member and asks him or her to answer the following question…

'What is (your name) like to work for?'

What do you think the team member would *really* say, speaking in all honesty?

_____

_____

_____

_____

_____

_____

_____

_____

You may, of course, have a range of different answers, depending on whether the team member in the lift was a 'Chris' or a 'Pat'.

Clearly, the brand experience that different people have of you is important: many people who start as a youngster in an organization create a brand experience of someone immature, gauche and low value due to their youth and lack of experience. Unfortunately for them, some of their more senior colleagues will have this brand experience in their heads for longer than is actually fair and this means that, in order to further their career, people need to move on to a new employer where they create a new brand experience as a competent, experienced professional with sound judgement. Such is life.

But on the other hand, if you are completely concerned about the brand experience you leave with other people it can be detrimental to you (and them).

Let's go back to 'Chris' again.

Chris is a member of your team whom you inherited from your predecessor. Chris is a bit lazy and slipshod, doing the bare minimum to keep out of trouble but never making much effort. Chris was allowed to get away with this under your predecessor. When you took over the team you were determined to help Chris improve. You instigated a weekly review of goals, actions and results but at the first one it was clear that Chris resented this intrusion. You didn't want Chris to think of you as a hectoring, nit-picking boss, so you backed off and allowed the status quo to continue. You reverted to a monthly review (like everyone else) and at that meeting you accept the excuses that Chris trots out to justify the missed targets and failures.

Your brand experience with Chris now is that you are a pushover!

Regardless of what you do with Pat, your brand with Pat is now that you are an inconsistent boss who allows people to coast with the result that Pat has to carry the dead wood that is Chris.

After a year, Pat leaves to go and work for a competitor and you are left with Chris....

The moral of the story is that you need to care about your brand experience with other people but you have to ensure that you keep a balance between being liked and being respected.

NEXT STEPS

In this chapter we have focused on your brand image: what this is and how, as a manager, you must keep careful control of it, especially in today's image-conscious world. You must be prepared to work hard at developing your brand constructively.

In Chapter 5, we will turn to the subject of how to manage your own learning and development.

TAKEAWAYS

What have you learned about your brand image from reading this chapter?

_____

_____

_____

_____

_____

_____

_____

_____

_____

_____

How will you change the way you manage your brand image in the future?

_____

_____

_____

_____

_____

_____

_____

_____

_____

_____

_____

MANAGING YOURSELF (IV): YOUR LEARNING AND DEVELOPMENT

5

 OUTCOMES FROM THIS CHAPTER

- Learn about the different types of learning.
- Develop your own action plan for your learning goals.

One way to generate and retain the respect of people around you is to learn and develop as a person, as a colleague and as a manager.

MANAGING YOUR DEVELOPMENT

COACHING SESSION 14

Your development at work: questionnaire

Before we go any further, answer the following questions:

1. What was the last thing I learned at work?

_____

_____

_____

_____

_____

_____

2. When was that?

_____

_____

_____

_____

_____

_____

3. How long did it take/how much effort was it to learn it?

_____

_____

_____

_____

_____

4. How did I learn it?

_____

_____

_____

_____

_____

5. (How) have I practised/used it since I learned it?

_____

_____

_____

_____

_____

6. How much difference has it made to my life/outputs/success/efficiency?

_____

_____

_____

_____

_____

_____

_____

7. Was it worth it? (question 3 above vs. question 6 above)

_____

_____

_____

_____

_____

_____

Look at the answers you have written for Coaching session 14.

1. *What was the last thing I learned at work?*

   Was it transitory or longer term? For example, 'transitory' may be a fact, such as last month's sales figures; you need to know them for now, but in two years' time they will be of little value. 'Longer term' might be the reasons that last month's sales figures were so high/low; this will be a valuable piece of knowledge for a longer period as it will give you a strong steer with regard to future actions.

2. *When was that?*

   You should be learning all the time; the reality is that we all are, but we often simply don't recognize it as learning, we put it down as 'experience'. The important thing about experience is not that you had it, but what you learned from it!

3. *How long did it take/how much effort was it to learn it?*

   Clearly, there is a difference here between learning that was 'spoon-fed' to you – for example the sales figures arriving on your desk in a tidy, summarized document – and learning that took some effort to discover, such as you rooting through prospect lists and forecasts, interviewing customers and having meetings to assess reasons for outcomes. So this could be anything from five minutes' reading an email to three days on a course; if it is the latter, then one would hope that you learned more than one thing!

4. *How did I learn it?*

5. This seems to replicate the comments above, but the important element here is to recognize the responsibility we all have for our own learning. If you haven't actually had to put much (or any) personal effort into learning something, then the likelihood is that you haven't really embedded the lesson – that is, you will soon forget it. Sadly, many senior executives get into this lazy habit. They have people to do so much for them that they don't really learn anything. (Also they have a vested interest in appearing to not need to learn anything; the fact that they already know it all is what justifies their position and salary.)

6. *(How) have I practised/used it since I learned it?*

   Your answer to this question is telling in two ways. First, it suggests the level of importance of the learning; if you haven't used or valued it, then it was either unimportant or certainly non-urgent. Alternatively, it suggests that you personally didn't value it. Have you ever seen your boss come back to the workplace after a management training course and manage in exactly the way he/she did before the course. If so, that is because he/she reckoned that they already knew it all.

7. *How much difference has it made to my life/outputs/success/efficiency?*

8. This is a critical question to put to yourself. If you learn something about the way you manage a particular member of staff, but it makes no difference, then it was pointless learning it. The sad fact is that often we learn the lesson but we fail to put it into practice, and therefore it makes no difference. (For example, we all know the theory of how to manage poor performance, but a great many managers don't actually do so because they are scared of accusations of bullying/falling foul of employment law/upsetting people's feelings and so on.)

9. *Was it worth it? (question 3 above vs. question 6 above)*

   This is the cost–benefit analysis. It is probably the hardest thing to do in some ways but also the easiest in others; it depends on the situation.

The day that you breathe your final breath will be the first time in your life that you don't learn something. Consequently, as a manager you will be constantly learning and developing. You can learn information and knowledge, and you can develop skills; some of this will be technical and some of it will be managerial. In terms of managerial learning, some of it will be generic management stuff and some will be self-awareness. Some of it will be information about your team and its individual members.

You will also learn lessons that relate to your long-term career. These are not necessarily things you'd put on your CV but the sort of 'life experience' lessons that will stand you in good stead in the longer term. Again, some of these will be to do with self-awareness: the things that you are good at and not so good at; the things you enjoy and don't enjoy; the things that are important or less important to you. Some will be about other people, not specific people, but generic lessons about human behaviour: common sense isn't actually that common and common courtesy isn't either, or the fact that all those people who were out to get you when you were a teenager, weren't.

You will also be learning things outside work, whether they relate to your relationships, parenting, hobbies and interests, or just what is going on in the world.

Answer the following questions:

COACHING SESSION 15

Your development outside work: questionnaire

Answer the following questions:

1. What was the last thing I learned outside work?

_____

_____

_____

_____

2. When was that?

_____

_____

_____

_____

3. How did I learn it?

_____

_____

_____

_____

_____

_____

_____

_____

_____

4. Is it something that I value enough to share with others?

_____

_____

_____

_____

_____

_____

_____

Take a while to reflect upon the answers you have written in Coaching session 15.

1. *What was the last thing I learned outside work?*

   If you can't think of anything that you have learned outside work, then perhaps you need to re-evaluate your life; it may well be that you have been learning but simply don't recognize it, but if you genuinely haven't learned anything for several months, you might want to question how happy you really are with this situation. It isn't wrong to not learn; but it is something that perhaps you ought really only be happy with if you are an centenarian who has truly made peace with your gods and are simply awaiting your turn to shuffle off this mortal coil.

2. *When was that?*

   See above.

3. *How did I learn it?*

It is possible that you learned this through a formal training course but probably more likely that it was through reading or TV or some form of experience. (See the section below for an investigation of 'experiential learning'.)

4. *Is it something that I value enough to share with others?*

Think about why this would matter in each instance. If you learn a lesson which you want to pass on to your children, family or community, then this suggests that it was a valuable lesson. On the other hand, if you learn a lesson that presents you with a massive competitive advantage over everyone else, you may decide to keep that learning to yourself. So whether you chose to share or guard your learning is not pertinent, but why you decided to do so is!

LEARNING

There are two fundamental ways of learning:

1. intentionally
2. intuitively.

Intentional learning

This is what happens when you deliberately set out to learn something, either through self-motivation or when told to do so. So where you book yourself on a course or your boss sends you on a course are the most common forms of intentional learning. Perhaps it is the most easily recognizable way in which most of us develop at work. However, we also have various other options open to us:

- There is a myriad of **e-learning modules** available, whether your employer has its own library or licence or whether you want to access paid, or free, e-learning on an individual and self-motivated basis.

- **YouTube** has 'how to' videos on pretty much every topic you can imagine, from how to display your late grandfather's war medals to how to create a great PowerPoint® presentation, and from how to use curling tongs to how to manage a person's poor performance.

- There are **'white papers'** and **articles** available from an enormous range of websites, available in most languages.

- There are **forums** where you can post a question or seek advice from a 'community of interest' – again, these range from Renault owners to HR professionals.

- Coming away from the virtual world, you can always **learn on the job**. This is generally reckoned to be less costly and more effective than 'book learning' and it will almost certainly be more tailored to working in your own organization. Notwithstanding that, it can also be a bit insular and introspective: you may learn the way it has always been done/known within this organization, but that could be either very out of date or simply not the best way to do something, just the 'house' way.

- You can also learn from **books** and **periodicals** (much as you are doing at this very moment).

- You can learn simply by asking someone their **advice** or **assistance**.

An important thing about intentional learning is to separate the learning from the solving of the 'problem'.

COACHING SESSION 16

Intentional learning vs. solving the problem

Read the following case study.

You need to get a spreadsheet to carry out a particular calculation in one specific cell, so you go to see Caroline who is the Excel queen and knows all that there is to know about spreadsheets. Caroline is busy but she is a very helpful person, so she takes time out of her busy schedule to quickly set up the spreadsheet for you, quickly talking you through how she does it. On completion, she emails the completed spreadsheet back to your inbox. You thank her and go back to your desk

Problem solved!

Have you actually learned anything and what will be the net result?

_____

_____

_____

_____

_____

_____

_____

_____

Well, of course, you have learned nothing. Caroline has done all the work, and the next time you come across the problem you will have to plead for her help again.

So there is a big difference between getting someone to 'help' us, and us actually learning something. Perhaps once we have been to see Caroline five times, for the same thing, we may start to remember how she did it as we looked over her shoulder and she rapidly moved the cursor around and hummed quietly to herself. This is actually intuitive learning, where we have learned almost by osmosis through repetition.

Intuitive learning

As we have just mentioned, we all tend to learn intuitively all the time but the problem is that it tends to take a lot longer. If you consider the old-fashioned approach to apprenticeships most of the learning was actually intuitive. For instance, an apprentice blacksmith spent pretty much the whole of his first year pumping the bellows, while the tradesman/artisan did all the metal heating, shaping and so on. This was partially to build up the youngster's muscles for the later career, but there was also an expectation that, just by watching and listening, the youth would pick up much of the trade. There were precious few 'lessons' and very little opportunity to try or practise. Full apprenticeships were often five or seven years of fifty-two, six-day weeks, eight or more hours a day.

Intuitive learning can also take place via actual practice, but in a vacuum away from any formal teaching or coaching. Consider a youngster learning how to use a hammer to put in nails. It is unlikely that most people actually get taught; they simply watch their dad or mum doing it and then attempt to replicate the action. After several tries, they may become quite proficient at the different aspects of the task: hitting the nail rather than the wood; hitting the nail rather than their fingers; driving the nail in with one or two strong blows, rather than tapping it in to place in tiny increments over several dozen blows. More likely is that the learner will become quite proficient at some aspects, but not all, and will not be aware that their technique is not as good as it could be (although they may be aware that the technique could be improved but don't know how).

LEARNING FROM EXPERIENCE

Learning from experience can take the form of intuitive learning but it can be speeded up by a simple three-step process (Figure 4.1).

Once you have completed stage 3, you do it again, only differently. Clearly, you may not have found the right or best way to do it differently, which is why the cycle then continues, 'If at first you don't succeed, try, try again'.

Let us consider for a moment the word used as a title on step 2 – 'Reflect':

Figure 4.1 Learning from experience

- 'Reflect' can mean to look backwards at something behind you – so you can look back at past experience and learn. By answering the questions in Coaching sessions 14 and 15, you were doing an element of just that; you were reflecting on past experiences. In fact, it is true to say that you can reflect on experience a long time ago and still learn something from them.

- 'Reflect' can be used in the sense used in 'It reflects well on Chris that she is prepared to try something new.' So trying things you have never done before with the primary intention of learning from the experience reflects well on your brand image.

- 'Reflect' is used in relation to your reflection – the concept of looking at yourself as others see you and coaching yourself rather than being solely reliant upon the guidance or criticism of others.

- 'Reflect' means 'to ponder' or 'consider', as in 'I shall reflect on that and give you an answer in the morning.' Being a thinking person is seldom a bad thing!

🗩🗩 COACHING SESSION 17

Reflect...

Before you read on, take another peek at the answers you wrote to Coaching sessions 14 and 15 and edit them as necessary.

So are we recommending only the formal learning of the kind where we book ourselves on to training courses or take MBAs at night school? Not at all! What we all need to do is to engage in more 'informal learning', but make it more deliberately intentional.

COACHING SESSION 18

Action plan: set your learning goals

Use the following grid to set yourself some learning and development goals to further your knowledge and skills over the coming year.

Work-based technical development		
What I want to learn (to do) and why	How I propose to learn it	When I propose to learn it by

Work-based managerial development		
What I want to learn (to do) and why	How I propose to learn it	When I propose to learn it by

Outside work learning (include family/parenting, societal/community, health and hobby development)		
What I want to learn (to do) and why	How I propose to learn it	When I propose to learn it by

Bonus section just for me! What I want to do, for sheer enjoyment and if I learn something along the way, then great! (e.g. visit somewhere exciting or do something challenging)

→ NEXT STEPS

In this chapter we have looked at the importance that paying attention to your own development and learning has in your role as manager, both in terms of refining your skills and acquiring new ones, and in providing a positive role model for your team.

In the next chapter we look at your morale and how you can manage the natural ups and downs of working life.

TAKEAWAYS

What have you learned about learning from reading this chapter?

_____

_____

_____

_____

_____

_____

_____

_____

_____

Sketch out what you consider to be the importance of learning for you, your team and your organization.

_____

_____

_____

_____

_____

_____

_____

_____

_____

_____

_____

_____

MANAGING YOURSELF (V): YOUR MORALE

 OUTCOMES FROM THIS CHAPTER

- Learn how to keep your morale on an even keel.

Your morale is your level of energy and attitude at any time. We all have good days and bad days; that is human nature. However, we have to behave as consistently as possible in order to remain effective members of society and effective managers. Crashing a train or strangling a member of staff is not considered acceptable just because you were feeling a bit off that day. This chapter looks at ways to maintain as much equilibrium in your morale as possible.

This topic is very pertinent in today's world, where the economic outlook remains uncertain, where budgets – personal, organizational and national – are tight, and global issues such as climate change, war and terrorism threaten our very future. It is really no wonder that people's morale seems to be a bit of an issue, even before one even considers individual 'bad days'.

Most chapters in this workbook so far have started with a diagnostic. This one doesn't, simply because we don't want to depress ourselves by seeing how negative we might be! Instead, we will start by looking at *avoiding* being negative.

AVOIDING NEGATIVE FEELINGS

Very few people are really 'negative', as in negative about everything, all of the time. Most people are negative about some things, but positive and happy about others; even gloom-prone teenagers can usually manage some enthusiasm about something, even if it is only about painting their bedroom black or contemplating how bad their life is!

This may seem a small and semantic point, but it is fundamental to recognizing that, for example, although someone is commonly known as the office misery, they have it in themselves to be positive about something. Therefore, making some effort to cheer up and look on the bright side is worth while. If you don't accept this principle, you are distinctly limited in the ways in which you can deal with the situation.

This chapter isn't defining 'negative' as genuine clinical depression. If you feel genuinely stressed out, check the table below for the classic warning signs:

Signs of stress that can lead to clinical depression	
Signs visible to others	Signs only manifesting themselves to the sufferer
Obviously poor judgement Seeing only the negative Moodiness, irritability and short temper Susceptibility to getting colds Agitation, inability to relax Changes in eating habits Isolating self from others Procrastination and/or neglect of responsibilities Need of alcohol, cigarettes or other drugs to relax Nervous habits such as nail-biting, pacing about, etc.	Memory problems Anxious or racing thoughts Constant worrying Inability to concentrate Changes in sleeping habits Aches and pains for no apparent reasons Diarrhoea or constipation Nausea or dizzy spells Chest pain or rapid heart rate Loss of libido Feeling overwhelmed A sense of isolation and loneliness.

If you suspect that some of these apply to you, and you are suffering from clinical depression, then stop reading this and seek professional help.

Instead, this chapter is aimed more at the tendency to become a stick-in-the-mud, a naysayer, a gloom-monger, a person who just seems to suck the joy out of the room and drag everyone down to their own glum level. If you are a manager and you have looked in the mirror and seen this face staring back at you, you can imagine the effect it has on the people you manage!

Usually this is just a short-term phenomenon; it is worth catching it in the bud and preventing it from becoming permanent and/or habitual.

Being 'negative' can manifest itself in two ways:

1. **Passive negativity** – this is 'Eeyore-like' behaviour where everything is just viewed as a hardship and a wasted effort, and where everything is met with a long face and a resigned sigh. 'Nothing is worth the effort but I'll go along with it for a quiet life.'

2. **Active negativity** – this is a militant refusal to put any effort into anything because of a heartfelt belief that it just won't work, a vocal refusal to accept that anyone else has a valid point of view or that anything will ever be made better. We aren't talking here about anything constructive; there is no alternative proposed, no willingness to 'try it and see' – this is purely negative. It is often a habit and is sometimes induced by the surroundings; there are many people who, at work, simply walk around all day with a long face, moaning about everything and sabotaging all efforts to make things better.

There are many people who simply don't recognize that:

- their life is not, in fact, awful *and*
- other people aren't totally useless.

According to a 2010 study carried out by the University of Michigan, there is a chemical called neuropeptide Y that is present in the brain of human beings. In people with a low level of this NPY (as it is more snappily called), there is an increased likelihood, in response to 'negative words', of a stronger activation of the prefrontal cortex, which is the bit of the brain that produces your emotional reactions. These same people reported a higher level of emotion in anticipation of pain.

It is anticipated that in time the scientists may be able to use this discovery to treat these symptoms, probably with drugs. However, you didn't buy this book to be told to wait for the drugs!

Instead, we are going to look at strategies and examples of ways that negativity has been turned around by both the negative individual themselves, and by the external influence of others. We are going to look at both home and at work.

DEALING WITH YOUR OWN NEGATIVITY

There are two fundamental questions that you need to consider:

1. Can you actually do anything about the things you are glum about?
2. What's the use of worrying?

Let's take these one at a time.

Can I do anything about it?

With you sitting at the centre of your own universe, 'things' can be categorized into five areas:

1. Things that affect you and you can control
2. Things that affect you and that you can influence
3. Things that affect you but you neither control nor influence
4. Things you are aware of, but that frankly don't affect you and are outside your sphere of influence
5. Things that don't directly affect you and about which you are in a state of blissful ignorance.

This can be shown graphically as a series of concentric rings (Figure 5.1):

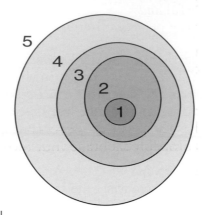

Figure 5.1 The circles of control

Frequently, we feel 'negative' (either passively or actively) precisely because, although things are bad, we feel powerless to do anything about it. For example:

5. Children are starving in Africa but you don't know about it... As your granny used to say: 'What the eye doesn't see, the heart doesn't grieve over', so it has no effect on you.

4. You are settling down to watch a show on TV and you catch the end of the preceding programme about children starving in Africa. You don't pay that much attention, so as soon as your show starts you put the African children from your mind.

3. You are settling down to watch a show on TV and you catch the end of the preceding programme about children starving in Africa, you watch it and felt sorry for them; but you don't live in Africa and you have no relatives in Africa so it doesn't affect you. You aren't the Overseas Development Minister and you don't work for Oxfam, so you may shed a tear but rationalize that it isn't your problem.

2. Every time you turn on the TV, you see images of children starving in Africa and the voice-over tells you that this famine is partially caused by global warming/climate change, and that you are partially responsible for because you leave your lights on overnight. If you turned off your lights each evening, things wouldn't be so bad next year.

1. You open your post in the morning and there is a letter from a charity asking you personally to sponsor this particular child for just £3 per month and if you do you personally will have saved little Joshua from a dreadful fate of child slavery/starvation/rickets.

Let's apply this to a more work-related situation. If you work for a large organization and you aren't on the board, then:

- You have no control over the planned changes to working practice;

- You may have some influence over the day-to-day changes planned in your immediate work area and if you want to then you can try to exert that influence;

- You do have control over the way you behave in response to changes imposed on you; you can debate them sensibly, rationally and openly, or you can sabotage them (and thus probably sabotage your own career as well!); *or*

- You can choose to actively support them or just go along with it; *or*

- If you are really unhappy, you can choose to resign and find a job elsewhere!

The first step is recognizing the futility of feeling responsible for something that is outside your control; get that sorted and you can learn to develop a 'devil-may-care' freedom from worry and stress.

Some days are finger-lickin' good and other days are just two-finger raisin' bad. If you are having a bad day, then try to do things to get yourself out of the doldrums:

- **'Count your blessings'** – just take a few minutes to think of the good things you have, even if they are common such as your health or the fact that you live in a country that isn't overrun by gun-toting warlords.

- **Have a *schadenfreude* moment** – compare your life/situation to other people who are worse off; you are bound to find someone who is having a less good time than you.

- **Look on the bright side** – for instance, actor and broadcaster Gryff Rhys Jones thinks that he is a lucky gambler; he always loses, so he doesn't get hooked and risk losing everything!

- **Listen to some music** that you find uplifting.

- **Get out into the daylight** – happy people are often referred to as having a 'sunny' disposition.

- **Get moving** – by getting your body moving, you generate hormones that make you feel more alive. If you can't walk or run, use a stress toy or do some isometric exercises *in situ*.

- **Have a primal scream!** A good yell also gets the blood flowing. (This can be merged with other suggestions in this list, for example that uplifting music – a good head-banging, air-guitar-strumming, chorus-yelling works wonders for many people.)

- **Give yourself a treat** – whether it is chocolate, a cup of coffee, a head massage or a game with the dog... whatever floats your boat.

- **Just do something different** – a change is as good as a rest!

- **Let go of the past**; you can't change it! Avoid mulling over failures and difficulties, injustices and betrayals. Learn from it and then get over it.

Being negative is detrimental to your professional life and career prospects. You can be as well qualified and competent as the next person, but if you look like a miserable individual you will find it very hard to get promoted or to win a new job. You will also find it very hard to motivate other people to want to achieve.

 COACH'S TIP

Be Tigger, not Eeyore

The former UK Prime Minister Tony Blair was an optimist and looked like one; he was upbeat, breathy and energetic. As 'Tigger'-like as a party-leading politician can be. He was elected to office repeatedly and had many followers who wouldn't traditionally have been Labour supporters. On leaving politics, he has used his natural enthusiasm to become a globally successful speaker commanding large fees just for appearing and opening his mouth.

Gordon Brown, who served first as Blair's Chancellor of the Exchequer (finance minister) and then as Prime Minister, on the other hand, was a dour, sombre, slower-talking individual who seldom seemed to be the bearer of good news and, even when he was, didn't seem to enjoy giving it! There were allegations that he bullied his staff and frequently lost his temper and ranted at people. On becoming Prime Minister, he was immediately embroiled in internecine warfare within the party and was rapidly rejected in the polls.

Being negative is also detrimental to your private life:

- It breaks up marriages – no one wants to live with a misery.

- It infects children – when youngsters are constantly reminded how pointless life is, it often creates a self-fulfilling prophesy.

- It deepens financial problems – banks don't like to lend money to people who expect everything to be appalling.

- It loses you friends – there is little fun in being with someone who is constantly moaning.

COACHING SESSION 19

Resource: build your morale

1. Count your blessings: List at least ten things that you have going for you.

2. Indulge your *schadenfreude*: list at least five people you know personally who have at least one problem that is greater than yours.

3. 'Look on the bright side of life': what is your single biggest 'problem' at present? What is the bright side of that problem?

4. What specific piece of music always lifts your spirits? (Once you have identified this, make sure you have it programmed on your iPod, MP3 player/mobile phone, etc.)

_____

_____

_____

_____

_____

5. What little treat always makes you feel a bit better?

_____

_____

_____

_____

_____

_____

 ## ONLINE RESOURCE

Boost your morale!

You can download an extra list of suggestions for boosting your morale by going to:

www.TYCoachbooks.com/Management

 ## NEXT STEPS

In this chapter we have looked at the importance of keeping your morale high, in terms of your professional life and personal life, and simple techniques to help you smooth out the natural highs and lows most of us experience.

We have now completed the chapters dealing with self-management. In the rest of the book, we will be building on this firm foundation to explore how we can best manage others.

👍 TAKEAWAYS

What have you learned about your morale from reading this chapter?

_____

_____

_____

_____

_____

_____

_____

_____

_____

_____

_____

How will you change the way you manage your morale in the future?

_____

_____

_____

_____

_____

_____

_____

_____

Thinking back across Chapters 2–6, why do you think the ability to self-manage is so important in a manager?

_____

_____

_____

_____

_____

_____

_____

_____

_____

_____

MANAGING OTHERS: INTRODUCTION

7

✔ OUTCOMES FROM THIS CHAPTER

- Reflect on the key questions of management.

- Learn about the 21 key qualities required by an excellent manager.

- Carry out self-assessment of your characteristics as a manager and – if you dare! – ask your team members to assess you.

Now we are ready to move on to look at the way you manage other people. In Chapters 7–13, we will be looking at the way you manage the people for whose performance you are formally responsible – your own 'team'. We will look at this generically at first and then there will be a short section to help you when you have to manage people who are situated remotely from you – a virtual, remote, decentralized or scattered team. In Chapter 14, we will go on to look at 'managing' people over whom you have no line authority; peers or internal departments, staff or contractors who report to someone else. In Chapter 15, we will also look at the way you 'manage' your boss!

Before we plunge deeply into theory, let's start with a little situational/self-analysis.

🗩🗩 COACHING SESSION 20

Why do you want to be a good manager?

Take five minutes to simply think about (no need to write the answers down) why it is important to you to be good at managing others.

Once you have exhausted that activity (if it took you 30 seconds, you may want to think again – it may well take 30 minutes over a period of a couple of days but it is a worthwhile activity), answer the questions below:

1. What is my definition of a 'team'?

_____

_____

_____

_____

_____

_____

_____

_____

2. What are the characteristics of a good 'team member'?

_____

_____

_____

_____

_____

_____

_____

_____

3. What are the characteristics of a good 'team leader/manager'?

_____

_____

_____

_____

_____

_____

_____

_____

Here are some possible thoughts you might have had about why you want to be good at managing others:

- I have to be good at managing **what other people think of me** because, if I'm poor or inconsistent at this, they may get an incorrect impression of me and my capabilities. This will lead to them having an inappropriate expectation. This could mean that I am never given the opportunity to reach my full potential or that I am setting myself up for a spectacular fall.

- I have to be good at managing other **people's individual workloads** because, if I'm poor or inconsistent at this, they will either resent me as a slave-driver or take advantage of me and reduce their productivity to the bare minimum.

- I have to be good at managing the **overall balance of the workloads** I hand out to people because, if I'm poor or inconsistent at this, some people will feel picked on and some people will feel untrusted.

- I have to be good at managing my **outgoing communication** with people because, if I'm poor at this, I will a) upset people by saying the wrong thing at the wrong time, b) say too much and bore people or confuse them with overload, or c) say too little and be accused of having a hidden agenda

- I have to be good at managing my **incoming communication** with people because, if I'm poor at this, I will a) make mistakes (because I wasn't listening), b) be thought of as aloof because I don't listen, or c) waste a huge amount of my time because I'm always available to listen to things that either I don't need to know or which I don't need to know at this particular time.

- I have to be good at managing **people's motivation** because, if I'm poor or inconsistent at this, I'll find that people who report directly to me will work only when I have them cornered like rats in a trap and am directly supervising their every move. Also, I'll find it very hard to get anyone over whom I have no direct authority to do anything for me.

- I have to be good at managing **people's relationships** with others because, if I'm poor or inconsistent at this, I'll end up with a dysfunctional work team and that will a) reflect badly upon me as a manager and b) mean that I have to spend more of my time trying to untangle big problems that grew out of petty squabbles that were allowed to get out of hand.

- I have to be good **overall** as a manager of others because I am already drawing a salary as a manager and I have bought this book, which suggests I want to further my career, and, if I'm poor or inconsistent at this, it is going to probably slow down my career quite considerably. In addition to this, good managers generally find life is quite easy: they can trust their staff because their staff respect them; good people come and work for them because staff talk about their managers; and senior managers promote good managers because they have higher achievement and lower staff turnover rates than poorer managers.

Now let's consider your written answers in Coaching session 20 in turn. They will tell you quite a lot about you, your team and the way you are currently managing.

WHAT IS A TEAM?

The received wisdom about the definition of a team is usually quite similar:

> *'A group of people with a full set of complementary skills required to complete a task, job, or project.'*
>
> www.businessdictionary.com/definition/team.html

> *'A team comprises a group of people or animals linked in a common purpose'*
>
> http://en.wikipedia.org/wiki/Team

> *'A team is a small number of people with complementary skills who are committed to a common purpose, performance goals, and approach for which they are mutually accountable.'*
>
> Katzenbach & Smith 1993

> *'People working together in a committed way to achieve a common goal or mission. The work is interdependent and team members share responsibility and hold themselves accountable for attaining the results.'*
>
> MIT Information Services and Technology

> *'A team is a group of people working together towards a common goal.'*
>
> Team Technology, 1995–2006

> *'A group in which members work together intensively to achieve a common group goal.'*
>
> Lewis-McClear & Taylor 1998

How did you get on with your definition? Did you get all the elements of a single common goal, complementary skills, interdependence, working together (as opposed to competing with each other), shared responsibility and shared accountability? These elements are important for a range of reasons:

Single common goal

This is important simply because, if it is not clearly understood and remembered at all times, people may well focus solely on their part rather than seeing this (slightly) bigger picture. In this instance, people can become 'jobsworths' and the team fragments because of infighting.

COACHING SESSION 21

Single common goal

When was the last time you reminded the whole team, all together, what the single common goal of the team was? Describe how you went about it.

_____

_____

_____

_____

_____

_____

_____

Complementary skills

Your management style will be different depending on whether you manage a team where the skills are common rather than complementary. For example: let's imagine that you manage a 'team' of service engineers. Each one has an identical skillset, an identical van, mobile phone, tablet computer and toolkit. They are tasked by a call centre and each goes independently to their allocated client's sites to install, diagnose and repair client-owned appliances. They are not actually a team in the formal definition. They work independently of one another and in many organizations they actually compete against each other. This is not 'wrong', but it will require a consciously different management style than the team that consists of the call centre operator who takes the customer's call and allocates an engineer, who in turn diagnoses the problem and is supported by the parts department warehouseman to get the right parts and the sales ledger clerk who invoices the customer.

⊙⊙ COACHING SESSION 22

Complementary skills

Is your 'team' one of complementary skills and, if so, when was the last time you actually consciously took a team-wide skills audit of what is needed and what is present – not just in terms of technical skills but also communication skills and behaviours? Describe how you went about it,

_____

_____

_____

_____

_____

_____

_____

Or is your 'team' one of common skills – a group that is called a team for reasons of similarity? If so, when was the last time you audited the skills they need and the skills each has in relation to their ability to function in this potential vacuum? Describe how you went about it.

_____

_____

_____

_____

_____

_____

_____

_____

Interdependence and working together

This is important because if your team members don't work together and recognize the interdependence they each have upon their teammates, you have a situation that was described by one manager in the finance industry as: "I don't so much manage a team as cope with a group of egos.'

COACHING SESSION 23

Interdependence

When was the last time you reminded your team of their interdependence each other? Describe how you went about it.

_____

_____

_____

_____

_____

_____

_____

_____

_____

_____

Accountability and responsibility

Many managers make a real mess of this matter.

- *Responsibility* needs to be delegated to each individual team member for their own element of the overall task. This means that each individual team member has a responsibility to use their initiative to ask for the resources they need to do their job, manage their own time, be considerate of their colleagues, look after their own contribution to health and safety, take responsibility for their own choices and check their own work.

- *Accountability* means that each individual team member is accountable (with forfeits and punishments, praise and rewards, as appropriate) for their own outputs and their contribution to the team's effort. It does not mean that individual team members can use 'I was just following orders' as an excuse for personal failure, nor does it mean that, if the team fails in its overall goal, that we can all just cry 'collective responsibility – it's not my personal fault' and walk away unscathed.

COACHING SESSION 24

Accountability and responsibility

What is your track record of managing poor performance among your team?

_____

_____

_____

_____

_____

_____

_____

_____

_____

_____

What is your track record of managing good and excellent performance among your team members?

_____

_____

_____

_____

_____

_____

_____

_____

_____

WHAT IS A GOOD TEAM MEMBER?

Ronald Riggio, the Professor of Leadership and Organizational Psychology at Claremont McKenna College, lists seven characteristics of a good 'team member':

1. A good team member is straightforward, honest and up-front. Teammates and the team leader can count on a good team member to tell them what's what, regardless of whether it is good news or bad news. A good team member will challenge a decision that he/she genuinely disagrees with.

2. A good team member shares the load equitably. There is a sense of fairness in the good team member. Note 'equity', not 'equality': newbies, people with genuine reasons to temporarily downshift and so on are allowed to take a commensurate workload.

3. A good team member can be relied on. She or he will give it 100 per cent to hit targets and deadlines.

4. A good team member gives and takes appropriate credit, and would never think of taking credit for someone else's work.

5. An important characteristic of effective work teams is complementary skills. Every member has areas of strength and some weak spots. A good team member provides some appropriate skill and/or knowledge that moves the team forward.

6. Teamwork is a social activity, so good team members are skilled, and tactful, communicators. They are both good listeners and good active communicators.

7. It is hard to follow a pessimistic leader, but easy to 'follow' a pessimistic team member. A good team member therefore has a positive, 'can do' attitude even when they challenging something that they genuinely believe needs to be challenged

In the book *Managing Teams for Dummies*, Marty Brounstein adds three more characteristics:

8. A good team member functions as an active participant in all team activities. They arrive at meetings prepared, they contribute and take an interest in the activities of their teammates.

9. A good team member solves problems, rather than dwells on problems, looking for them or blaming others for them. They get straight to the matter of solving it and then evade meeting it again.

10. They are committed to the team rather than just concentrating on their role in isolation. That doesn't mean that they are 'cheerleaders', but that they actively support the team as a whole.

COACHING SESSION 25

A good team

Did you get all these characteristics in your answers? What did you miss?

_____

_____

_____

_____

_____

_____

_____

How does your team stack up?

_____

_____

_____

_____

_____

_____

_____

How many of your team members exhibit all these (the ones above from the 'experts' and your own list) characteristics all the time, and, if they don't, what have you done about it to date?

_____

_____

_____

_____

_____

_____

_____

_____

_____

_____

_____

WHAT IS A GOOD MANAGER? THE KEY OF THE DOOR TO GOOD MANAGEMENT

Everyone has an opinion about what makes a good manager. Below is a summary of a range of different opinions culled from web searches, live focus groups of staff and managers and reading different management thinkers. They have been broken into five categories but are pretty generic, regardless of where a manager works and how many people there are in his or her team. I've called this list 'The key of the door to good management' because the bingo slang for 21 is 'key of the door'.

Traits that make people 'look up' to you as a person rather than kowtow to your rank

1. **A sense of agency/proactivity:** No manager can motivate others if he/she doesn't self-motivate. The ability to get yourself going, and take charge of things that are within your sphere of influence, is a therefore a crucial characteristic for any manager.

2. **Realistic optimism:** A manager's positive attitude can inspire the whole team, and sometimes inspiration is just about all there is or all that was needed to get a team performing

3. **Reliability:** Every manager should be dependable and reliable; promises are worth nothing until they are kept. Your bosses, your team, your customers and your peers need to know that you can be counted on.

4. **Self-belief:** A good manager believes in himself/herself – without that, why would anyone else believe in them? Self-belief enables a manager to make decisions with confidence, and that shows to others. Confidence rubs off on others and can be of untold benefit.

5. **Equilibrium:** As a manager, you can't afford to break down or blow up when the pressure is on. Remaining calm and doing what needs to be done is essential in a good manager.

6. **Integrity:** Your team need to know that you will fight for them; your customers need to know that you will do what is right; and your bosses need to know that you will use your judgement wisely

7. **Adaptability:** It is said that the only constant is change; as a manager, you have to be able to make change happen and that starts with you. You also have to accept that hardly any plan ever goes completely by the book; thinking on your feet and adjusting, adapting and improvising are key skills

Business characteristics

A degree of business acumen is important for any manager whether they manage a commercial department, a team of public servants or even a company of soldiers. While you may not need to be a full-time deal-maker, a grasp of the basic principles of cost efficiency is really beneficial.

8. **Organizational skill:** A good manager needs to keep track of targets, performance, goals, assignments, development, customers, budgets, etcetera etcetera. You can't be a good manager if these things keep surprising you.

9. **Sector knowledge:** A good manager understands their industry so that they can answer questions and perform their work more effectively.

10. **Respect for the law:** Being a manager lays you open to all manner of responsibilities – health and safety, employment law, consumer rights, professional liability... the list is constantly changing. A good manager doesn't have to be a legal expert but an understanding of the basics and how/where to find the detail is important.

11. **Willingness and ability to delegate:** An effective manager knows that some tasks need to be delegated. You should be able to identify:

    i. team members who will benefit from the experience and responsibility

    ii. tasks that may benefit from being delegated to specific people

    iii. occasions when it is appropriate to delegate tasks.

12. **'Political nous':** A good manager should know how the formal and the informal hierarchy works within the organization; he/she should also know how the office politics affects their subordinates. Everybody hates office politics, but they are here to stay!

Communication characteristics

Most poor managers are poor communicators in some way shape or form. There are lots of facets to this.

13. **Verbal articulacy:** A good manager can get a message across effectively, quickly and without causing undue offence even when that message is unwelcome (but justifiably critical) feedback. This includes verbalizing clear and unambiguous instructions.

14. **Written communication:** Clarity in emails, memos, texts, reports and formal documents is vital, whether it is three lines or three hundred pages.

15. **Formal presentation skills:** As a good manager, you should know how to speak publicly, enunciating your words, and concisely communicating your ideas, whether in a one-to-one interview, a formal meeting or a video presentation, whether to team members, senior management, customers or even a tribunal hearing. This includes planning and working with others on team presentations.

16. **Active listening:** One of the most important communication skills for a manager is listening. By listening you understand and by understanding you have the foundation for your own decisions and actions. This includes listening when someone is giving you feedback about yourself ... especially when that person is a member of your team rather than your boss!

Relationship characteristics

Relationships matter when you are a manager. You will need to know how to manage relationships between yourself and your team, as well as manage the relationships among your team members.

17. **Customer service:** A good manager relates to customers (be they internal or external, paying or not, B2B or B2C) and sees things from their perspective. This allows you to manage, more effectively, the people who deliver the service to the customers.

18. **Peacemaker:** A good manager needs to be able to act as a mediator or arbitrator between team members, between a team member and a client, or between a boss and a team member. He/she will understand the nature of conflict and therefore be able to avoid most (no one can avoid all) conflicts personally as well as being able to help people to calmly find common ground and reach mutually acceptable solutions.

19. **Collaborative and non-hierarchical:** A good manager is able to function as part of a team. He/she is willing to work with others, to make sensible compromises and to 'roll up their sleeves' and to 'get their hands dirty', where necessary. A good manager also recognizes that their rank does not automatically make them a fount of all knowledge and the owner of the best ideas.

20. **Values others:** A good manager values the team and each of its individual members ... and makes sure they know it appropriately. Valuing a person can be as simple as thanking them for a decent job or praising them to their face or to others. It can also include promoting them, rewarding them and giving them a (deserved) bonus/award. It also includes pointing out their failings and helping them to improve if they are not performing well.

21. **Respect:** A good manager respects his or her team members – their effort, their knowledge and skill, their right to a home life and their right to opinions. In return, the good manager will get respect back ... even if they don't get love.

COACHING SESSION 26

The key of the door to good management

You need to have each of the 21 characteristics in fairly high order if you want to be a good manager… How do you match up? The form below enables you to carry out a self-assessment. Score it as honestly as you possibly can.

	Characteristic	Score where 1 is completely disagree and 10 is agree completely
1	I am always proactive and show a sense of agency.	1 2 3 4 5 6 7 8 9 10
2	I am permanently realistically optimistic.	1 2 3 4 5 6 7 8 9 10
3	I am totally reliable.	1 2 3 4 5 6 7 8 9 10
4	I demonstrate my self-belief at all times.	1 2 3 4 5 6 7 8 9 10
5	I always act with equilibrium and calm.	1 2 3 4 5 6 7 8 9 10
6	I behave with total integrity in all things.	1 2 3 4 5 6 7 8 9 10
7	I am adaptable and cope with life's challenges.	1 2 3 4 5 6 7 8 9 10
8	I am 100 per cent organized and efficient.	1 2 3 4 5 6 7 8 9 10
9	I have a perfect knowledge of my chosen sector.	1 2 3 4 5 6 7 8 9 10
10	I make sure we all stay within the law every time.	1 2 3 4 5 6 7 8 9 10
11	I am a great delegator.	1 2 3 4 5 6 7 8 9 10

	Characteristic	Score where 1 is completely disagree and 10 is agree completely
12	I understand and work around 'office politics' like a pro.	1 2 3 4 5 6 7 8 9 10
13	I can get a message across well verbally every time.	1 2 3 4 5 6 7 8 9 10
14	I can get a message across well in writing.	1 2 3 4 5 6 7 8 9 10
15	I'm fantastic in front of an audience.	1 2 3 4 5 6 7 8 9 10
16	I'm a great listener.	1 2 3 4 5 6 7 8 9 10
17	I always empathize with customers.	1 2 3 4 5 6 7 8 9 10
18	I never get into conflicts and I'm the best at helping others get out of theirs.	1 2 3 4 5 6 7 8 9 10
19	I'm a 'team members' team manager'.	1 2 3 4 5 6 7 8 9 10
20	I always give credit where credit is due, without fail.	1 2 3 4 5 6 7 8 9 10
21	I respect each and every member of my team and they know it.	1 2 3 4 5 6 7 8 9 10
		Total out of 210

Look at the scores you have given yourself:

Where your score is between 1 and 4, you really need to be seeking to improve as a matter of urgency. Look back the section on managing your development in Chapter 5, and decide what, when and how you might go about doing this as a matter of urgency.

Where your score is between 5 and 7, you are achieving reasonably well, you are probably exhibiting the characteristic fairly well or most of the time. This is therefore something that can be improved but it is a lower priority. Start to plan ways to improve over the coming year.

Where your score is 8 or 9, you should be a pretty good boss to work for, but there's no room for complacency.

Where you have scored a 10... really? Are you kidding yourself? There is one sure fire way to find out.

ONLINE RESOURCE

The key to the door of good management

You can download a file named 'The key of the door to good management'. In this file you will find:

- a questionnaire that you can give to your team members so that they can score you on the same criteria that you have just scored yourself on

- a set of suggestions for you with regard to administering this questionnaire.

This is a valuable exercise, as most of us have a self-image which is not entirely aligned to the image our staff have of us. It is also true that, as in the section about your brand experience Chapter 4, not everyone will have a common view of you. This may be something that you expect, understand and are comfortable with. However, it may be that you are blissfully unaware that one member of your team has a view of you that is completely at odds with your expectations. In that instance, you will want to find out and to investigate where you are going wrong.

www.TYCoachbooks.com/Management

NEXT STEPS

In this chapter I asked you to reflect on some of some key questions of management:

- what makes a good team?

- what makes a good team member?

- What makes a good team leader?

We have focused, above all, on the key qualities – 21 no less – that you need to have to have or acquire if you want to be an excellent manager. This may sound like a tall order, but in the following chapters I am going to show you how to get there… First, in Chapter 8 we will look at how you can focus more of your time on managing people, rather than on the other 'stuff' that can sometimes keep you hidden away from your team.

TAKEAWAYS

Based solely on the diagnostics in this chapter (whether you have carried out a team-member opinion survey or not), what are you going to do to improve?

Things I will learn (and by when)

1 _____

2 _____

3 _____

4 _____

5 _____

Things I will start doing (and by when)

1 _____

2 _____

3 _____

4 _____

5 _____

Things I must to stop doing (and by when)

1 _____

_____

2 _____

_____

3 _____

_____

4 _____

_____

5 _____

_____

Things I do that I need to do more of (and by when)

1 _____

_____

2 _____

_____

3 _____

_____

4 _____

_____

5 _____

_____

Things I do that I need to make an effort to do less of (and by when)

1 _____

_____

2 _____

_____

3 _____

_____

4 _____

_____

5 _____

_____

_____

YOUR DAY-TO-DAY MANAGEMENT ACTIVITIES

8

 OUTCOMES FROM THIS CHAPTER

- Learn how to refocus more of your time on people management.
- Use a checklist to help you structure your people-oriented management activities.

Most managers in the modern world, whether in the public or the private sector, spend a lot of their time doing 'their own work' rather than managing their people. For example, if you manage a shop, you probably spend a rather large proportion of your time on the floor dealing with customers, on the phone (or computer) ordering stock, checking takings and balancing stock sold with receipts, organizing point-of-sale materials, planning promotions and dealing with local marketing. Figure 7.1 is a job description for a retail store manager downloaded from the Internet.

From this job description, you can see that only three out of the 15 different 'duties' actually relate to staff; all the others relate to other activities. So, it could be surmised that only 20 per cent of the role is about managing people, while 80 per cent is about managing 'stuff'. If we accept that, then it would be reasonable to infer that a manager will spend only 20 per cent of the day (or about an hour and a half) with members of the team.

This, however, is a gross simplification and a distortion of the facts; if a manager is effectively delegating 'stuff' tasks to appropriate people, then he/she can spend a far higher proportion of his or her time on number 3: '...coaching, counselling and disciplining employees; planning, monitoring and appraising job results'. This action will bring the manager closer to the staff, allow him or her to develop and grow the staff and their abilities, and create a more sustainable team to fulfil all the other responsibilities.

Retail Store Manager

Job duties:

1. Completes store operational requirements by scheduling and assigning employees; following up on work results.

2. Maintains store staff by recruiting, selecting, orienting and training employees.

3. Maintains store staff job results by coaching, counselling and disciplining employees; planning, monitoring and appraising job results.

4. Achieves financial objectives by preparing an annual budget; scheduling expenditures; analysing variances; initiating corrective actions.

5. Identifies current and future customer requirements by establishing rapport with potential and actual customers and other persons in a position to understand service requirements.

6. Ensures availability of merchandise and services by approving contracts; maintaining inventories.

7. Formulates pricing policies by reviewing merchandising activities; determining additional needed sales promotion; authorizing clearance sales; studying trends.

8. Markets merchandise by studying advertising, sales promotion and display plans; analysing operating and financial statements for profitability ratios.

9. Secures merchandise by implementing security systems and measures.

10. Protects employees and customers by providing a safe and clean store environment.

11. Maintains the stability and reputation of the store by complying with legal requirements.

12. Determines marketing strategy changes by reviewing operating and financial statements and departmental sales records.

13. Maintains professional and technical knowledge by attending educational workshops; reviewing professional publications; establishing personal networks; participating in professional societies.

14. Maintains operations by initiating, co-ordinating and enforcing programme, operational and personnel policies and procedures.

15. Contributes to team effort by accomplishing related results as needed.

Figure 7.1 Sample manager's job description

👥👥 COACHING SESSION 27

Making time to manage people: checklist

Here is a checklist that may help you to escape from your office or from behind your spreadsheet, and get out and spend more time managing your people rather than managing 'stuff'.

DAILY 'TO DO' ITEMS (Do each one, every working day and at least once.)	Done it?
Say a cheerful and happy 'hello' to everyone who is in your team.	☐
Say 'thank you' for every job done well for you by a team member.	☐
Say 'well done' when you see a team member do something right (go out and deliberately look for someone doing something right!).	☐
Catch a member of your team at a quiet moment away from their workstation and spend five minutes asking their opinion of something relevant (your own products or service, a new member of staff, the competition, the future of the economy or sector).	☐
Take an interest in one of your team member's life outside work.	☐
WEEKLY 'TO DO' ITEMS (Do each one, every working week at least once.)	**Done it?**
Have a five-minute catch-up with each one of your team based on how they are getting on, have they got all the resources and support they need to do their job, what is going well at the moment and what is presenting challenges.	☐
Spend whatever time is necessary reacting to the outcomes of 1 above.	☐
Take ten minutes to trawl the Internet and download and read news and articles for your sector/specialization.	☐
Delegate at least one task that is developmental for the person to a member of your team (see Chapter 9).	☐
Hold a formal team activity that is inclusive for all the team, delegate the running of this to a rota of team members (see Chapter 10).	☐
MONTHLY 'TO DO' ITEMS (Do each one every working month at least once.)	Done it?
Review every team member's work targets and objectives with them to ensure that there are no nasty surprises.	☐
Schedule at least one team member on to some form of learning activity that is developmental for them or for the organization (see Chapter 10).	☐
Hold an informal team activity that is inclusive for all team members and host this yourself (see Chapter 10).	☐
Seek some feedback from at least one member of the team relating to your performance as the team manager. Respond to this feedback by scheduling learning activity that is appropriate.	☐

Report to your boss at least one success story from your team and its activity.	☐
QUARTERLY 'TO DO' ITEMS (Do each one each quarter at least once.)	**Done it?**
Hold a one-to-one with each team member to discuss and action the elements listed in table on 'Managing individual performance' in Chapter 11).	☐
Administer, analyse and report to the team the teamworking tool in Chapter 10.	☐
Manage a developmental learning or communication session for all the team based on the organizational needs rather than individual needs (e.g. a presentation from another department about their work or a 'state of the nation' presentation from a senior manager).	☐
Recommend a worthy person from your team for a commendation, award, promotion or bonus.	☐
Get some PR for your team and its activities in some form of trade/ national/local press or website.	☐

→ NEXT STEPS

In this short chapter we have looked at how you can give greater focus to team or person management and I have provided a useful checklist to help you to do so. In the following chapters we will hone in on many of the areas mentioned in the checklist, starting with the tricky subject of delegation.

👍 TAKEAWAYS

If you are already a manager, look at your current job description – how much of it is about management of 'stuff' and how much about management of people? Write down the people management components here.

_____

_____

_____

_____

_____

_____

_____

_____

_____

Describe how you currently divide your time between people and stuff management. Do you think you have got it about right?

_____

_____

_____

_____

_____

_____

_____

_____

_____

_____

After reading this chapter, how would you consider changing the way you manage the people in your team?

_____

_____

_____

_____

_____

_____

_____

_____

_____

_____

DELEGATING SUCCESSFULLY

✔ OUTCOMES FROM THIS CHAPTER

- Learn about the barriers to delegation and how to overcome them.
- Understand why effective delegation is a core management skill.
- Develop an action plan for delegation.

Delegating is a key skill of any good manager; sadly it is also one that many people find difficult for a range of different reasons.

COACHING SESSION 28

Obstacles to delegation

Let's have a little brainstorm of all the reasons why some managers don't delegate or don't delegate well.

The challenge is to identify ten different reasons:

1 _____

_____

_____

_____

_____

2 _____

_____

3

4

5

6

7

8

9

10

Overleaf is a 'stock answer' to this challenge.

Reasons why managers don't delegate or don't delegate well are:

- I don't trust anyone to do this as well as I can.

- It is quicker to do it myself than give someone instructions and then wait for them to do it and then go and check it.

- My boss gave this responsibility to *me* and therefore I must do it.

- If my staff could do this, it would make me dispensable, so I'd better keep the ability to myself.

- If I try to delegate this, people will think I'm offloading my work and being lazy.

- This is a business-critical task and it should be done by me to demonstrate this task's high importance.

- This is a really high-profile task so I should be the one who gets all the kudos and PR that goes with being seen to do it.

- I really enjoy doing this; it is one of the best parts of my day/week/year.

- This job relies on other people supporting it. If I ask someone to do it who has less authority, then they won't get the support – I'd be condemning them to failure.

- My staff aren't paid to do this, but I am.

- I should lead by example so I have to do it.

- If I delegate this to a particular member of my team, other people will either think I'm picking on them or they will think that they are 'teacher's pet', so it will be detrimental to team spirit.

- My people are already all overworked so, if there is any extra work to do, it is better that I do it myself, even if I have to work extra hours. (Also included here is the unacceptability of authorizing overtime for staff.)

- No one in the team has the ability to do this so I can't delegate it.

- I've tried to delegate this task but each time I try the person says that they can't do it.

Did you get all the 'stock answers'? How often have you used any or all of these?

WHY DELEGATE?

Let's consider the benefits of delegating tasks.

A staff member:

- learns a new skill or practices a skill

- gets some extra responsibility

- proves their capability above and beyond their day-to-day role

- gets a change of scenery and something new or different to do

- is seen by others as being appreciated for their trustworthiness and ability

- may perhaps see for themselves that life as a manager is not all a bed of roses

- prepares for the time when this task is an everyday responsibility for them (i.e. it lessens the chance that they will be promoted to a responsibility that is beyond their competence).

The manager will:

- benefit from the time that is freed up by not having to do the job

- benefit from demonstrating trust in the team member

- benefit from increasing the skill levels within the team – this will make for more flexibility of scheduling and manpower planning

- be able to signal to employees that they are appreciated for their ability and motivation

- be able to test employees' ability and motivation in a real-life way rather than making a judgement that could be wrong and certainly will be debated. See the coaching session below.

COACHING SESSION 29

Case study: Mike

Tony managed a team that included Mike. In Tony's view, although Mike was perfectly competent, he had an inflated opinion of his own ability and skill. He also was known to denigrate Tony and question many of his decisions behind his back. Mike was also someone who was quite big on 'workers' rights and discrimination', so Tony was reluctant to tackle Mike head on about his attitude and behaviours. Mike's attitude was becoming divisive.

With the theme of delegation in mind, what would you do in Tony's place?

_____

_____

_____

_____

_____

_____

Tony decided to delegate the control of one of his own routine tasks to Mike. He offered Mike help and support to do this, as it was a bigger job than Mike had ever managed, but Mike was supremely confident. Tony left Mike to it.

Mike screwed it up completely, entirely due to his own failings and his blind self-confidence. After some bluster and attempts to blame everyone but himself, Mike accepted in hindsight that actually Tony's job wasn't easy and that he, Mike, wasn't ready to be promoted.

The lesson learned, Tony forgave Mike and the situation improved immediately. Mike went on to eventually succeed Tony and have a successful career.

COACHING SESSION 30

Your own case study

From your own experience as a manager or of being managed, describe three instances where delegation has had a beneficial effect on 1) the manager 2) a team member and 3) the team.

1. The manager

_____

_____

_____

_____

_____

_____

_____

2. The team member

_____

_____

_____

_____

_____

_____

_____

_____

3. The team

_____

_____

_____

_____

_____

_____

_____

HOW TO DELEGATE

Look back at the list of why managers don't delegate. Not including the 'political' reasons, such as protecting your own job or grabbing the enjoyable jobs or the kudos, there are probably four 'affinity groups' that the reasons fall into:

1. **Skill** – the manager doesn't believe that the team member has the skill to do the job. (This may be a factual truth or a judgement by the manager.) The team member may also lack self-belief that he/she has the skill.

2. **Time** – the manager may perceive that the team member hasn't the time to take on the task. Alternatively, the manager may feel that he/she hasn't got the time to delegate the task or that the task will take the team member longer to achieve, and that is something that the deadline won't allow.

3. **Authority** – the manager may perceive that it will undermine his or her authority if this (or any) task is delegated. Or that the task requires a level of authority which is above the team members.

4. **Responsibility** – This is the matter of trust: 'If you want a job doing properly, do it yourself.'

You will notice that the initial letters of the four groups spell out the acronym STAR.

To overcome all these barriers to delegation, it is imperative to ensure that you delegate in a way that gives the person the skill, time, authority and responsibility for fulfilling the task effectively.

Skill

There is a balancing act to achieve in this area. If a person has never done something, then how can you, or they, know whether they have the ability to do it? You can't, and neither can they! So the balancing act is one of faith – do you have faith in their ability and do they have faith in their own ability?

From your point of view, this will probably be based on previous experience with the individual and with team members in general. If this person has proved a serial disaster in the past, you are unlikely to have faith in the likelihood of success on this occasion. Or if your general experience suggests that only you are skilled, and everyone else is inept, then you are similarly unlikely to entrust a job (or delegate it) to someone else.

From the point of view of the person to whom you are trying to delegate a task, a large element of this will be based on their perception of the personal consequences of failure. If the consequences of them messing up are high, then they will be unlikely to want to take on the task.

So, first you need to show faith, and second you need to ensure that the consequences of failure are lessened. This latter can be done by:

- ensuring that adequate time for the outcome to be properly checked before it is critical
- coaching the individual during completion of the task to help avoid failure
- delegating in small increments so that each element can be checked before the next (dependent) element is started
- delegating non-business-critical tasks first and slowly working up
- assuring that the individual recognizes that you have 'done' the four things above
- assuring the individual that you will not hold it against them unduly if they fail.

COACHING SESSION 31

Learned dependence

Reflect for a few minutes on what you think the term 'learned dependence' might mean and how it might relate to the topic of delegation (or lack of it).

Write down your ideas here:

'Learned dependence' is a condition where an individual has learned, through past experience (either their own or observed/reported), that being dependent is of benefit to them. Look at the following instances:

1. A manager tasks a team member to do a job. The team member hasn't started the job and the manager asks how it's going. The team member says that they haven't started yet, and the manager says: 'OK, don't worry; I'll do it.' The team member has got away with not doing a job and learns that a short delay is all that is needed to avoid the extra work.

2. The manager tasks a team member to do a job. The team member starts the job and the manager intervenes, saying: "You don't want to do it like that. Here, let me show you.' The team member stands back idly while the manager does job. The team member learns that it is seldom worth starting a delegated job.

3. The manager tasks a team member to do a job. The team member starts doing job, but stops and comes and tells manager that there is a problem. The manager either carries on as in example 2 above or, being very busy, tells the team member to go and get on with something else, until the manager is free. The deadline looms, and the manager does job quickly as time is now short. Once again the team member has got away with it, and has learned that identifying a 'problem' early gets you out of the effort.

4. The manager tasks a team member to do a job. The team member totally 'screws up' the job – this could be either accidental or deliberate; people learn that, if you make yourself untrusted, you avoid being delegated to. The manager has to undo the mess and consequently never asks that team member to do the job again.

5. If number 4 happens more than once there is an increased likelihood that the manager will never trust *any* team member to do *any* job; thus it becomes more likely that the manager will revert to examples 1, 2 and 3, so the whole thing becomes a vicious circle.

Time

Clearly, as a manager you need to ensure that, when you delegate a task, you consider 'time'. This needs to be done in four ways:

1. You need to make enough time for you to **explain the requirements of the task** to the person in adequate detail for them to have a good understanding of the objective and how they should achieve it. It will take time to delegate a task properly, but the amount of time saved in the longer run virtually always makes it worthwhile. As the old adage says, 'A stitch in time saves nine.'

2. You need to set aside enough time for the team member to **fulfil the task**, bearing in mind that they may have a lower level of skill at this stage, so it may take them longer than it might take you.

3. You need to set aside enough time for **checking the outcomes** to ensure that they are to an acceptable standard. (This can be time either for you or the individual to check, depending on the task and the individual.)

4. You need to ensure that this is **the 'right' time for them to be taking on the task**. This could be:

   - the right time in terms of their career/experience, as in 'Chris, now is the right time for you to be taking on more responsibility, so I'd like to delegate this task to you...'

   - the right time of the day or week, as in 'Chris, you have a couple of hours to spare, so I'd like to delegate this task to you...'

   - right time for the individual, as in 'Chris, you've been doing a really vital but boring job for the last two days checking those figures, so now I'd like to delegate something a lot more exciting...'

- the right time for you and the rest of the team (for example Tony's delegation to Mike in the case study earlier in the chapter).

- the right time for you, as in 'Chris, I'm going on holiday in July and I'm going to put you in charge while I'm away. To help prepare you for this and to allow me to be confident while I'm away, I'd like to delegate...'.

😐😐 COACHING SESSION 32

Time

From your own experience either as a manager or of being managed, describe a delegation situation where time was a crucial factor. Into which of the four categories above did it fit?

Write down your ideas here:

_____

_____

_____

_____

_____

_____

_____

_____

_____

_____

_____

Authority

Never delegate in secret! Always ensure that everyone who may come into contact with the person, and everyone upon whom the person may rely, is fully aware that they are acting on your authority, and that they have the power vested in them, by you, to receive the support they need. Think of it as if you are giving the person a 'deputy's badge' that clearly marks them out as having that right. This will usually mean sending out some form of communiqué to people within the organization, so make sure you do this in good time. You may occasionally have to reinforce this either because of staff changes or information overload.

Responsibility

As a manager, it is and remains your responsibility to ensure that many things are done. That means that you are responsible only for ensuring that they are done, not necessarily doing them yourself. Consequently, you can delegate the task while remaining responsible for the outcome and achievement. What you do is make the person to whom you delegate it responsible to you, while you remain responsible to the organization.

This is critical if you are to avoid falling foul of 'learned dependence'. There *must* be clarity of obligation, duty, reward or censure for delegation to be effective. If a person sees a delegated task as thankless, then they will see it, not as 'delegated', but as 'dumped'. If a person knows that they are not going to be held responsible for their actions, then they are less likely to take it as seriously as necessary; this can manifest itself by procrastination or simply making a half-baked effort.

COACHING SESSION 33

Responsibility

From your own experience either as a manager or of being managed, describe a delegation situation where responsibility was a crucial factor.

Write down your ideas here:

_____

_____

_____

_____

_____

_____

_____

_____

_____

_____

_____

Delegation can be used by a manager for a number of different purposes:

- To give a reward to a person for good performance. You can delegate an enjoyable task as a reward;

- To give public kudos to a person for good performance. You can delegate a high-profile task as a visible reward/public show of appreciation or support;

- To prove that a task is complex to a 'Mike' (see Coaching session 29); this could be a low-value task or a high-value task, but you would obviously use your judgement regarding the consequences;

- To prove to a person that they are capable of more than their current job role, thus boosting their confidence and self-esteem;

- To free up manager time for other things;

- To develop an individual's skill and knowledge level for the purpose of developing their career;

- To develop a wider skill base in the team as a whole to give the manager greater flexibility in workload scheduling;

- To provide more 'enrichment', change of scenery and variety to team members;

- To achieve a more equitable workload among the team members;

- To prepare for and allow the team manager or specific team members to take breaks from work, be they for training events, holidays, sickness or sabbaticals.

⧉ COACHING SESSION 34

Action plan: delegation

Complete the following action plan to help you delegate better.

Task	To whom	What do I do to ensure they have a STAR?
What tasks from my current 'to do' list shall I delegate to members of my team?		

What routine tasks from my job description will I regularly delegate (either always to one person or to a rota)?		
What task will I delegate to someone in the team … a) for their personal skill development		
b) to bring their workload up to an equitable level		
c) to help them understand my role		
d) to test them to prove a point to them		

e) to test them to prove a point to others		
What delegation will I do to level the workload generally in the team?		

THE END OF DELEGATION

If you delegate a task, you will usually retain the final quality-check to sign off the final outcome. If you delegate the task regularly and consistently to the same person you should, after a suitable period of success by that person, consider making the task a formal part of their job description. At that point, you should also give serious consideration to delegating the final quality-check to the individual and empowering them in this area rather than retaining the final 'rubber stamp'. This has two benefits:

1. It is the final statement of trust and faith in the individual.

2. It takes away one of the last delays in the task – the time it spends sitting in your metaphorical in-tray waiting for you to say yea or nay. This delay, multiplied for every task, is frequently the reason that organizational procedures take a matter of weeks rather than hours!

→ NEXT STEPS

In this chapter we have looked at the thorny area of delegation – a core skill that is often lacking in even otherwise competent managers. Delegation is crucial to a team's efficiency and effectiveness, frees up the manager's time, progresses team members' skills and careers, and enhances the vitally important spirit of trust and collaboration within the team.

It is to the topic of team spirit that we turn to next.

TAKEAWAYS

What have you learned about your own delegating skills from reading this chapter?

_____

_____

_____

_____

_____

_____

_____

_____

_____

_____

How will you change the way you manage delegation in the future?

_____

_____

_____

_____

_____

_____

_____

_____

_____

_____

_____

Describe what you think is the importance of good delegation for your organization as a whole.

_____

_____

_____

_____

_____

_____

_____

_____

_____

_____

BUILDING AND MAINTAINING A TEAM

10

OUTCOMES FROM THIS CHAPTER

- Learn about Tuckman's Stages of team formation.
- Understand how to manage team formation effectively.
- Understand the importance of maintaining team spirit or 'health' through active assessment.
- Try out some useful tools for building your team.

In any disaster movie, you will see a group of people with a common objective – probably to survive, escape, reach safety or similar. What you will see is the group go through various stages of development to meld eventually into some sort of 'team', even where there was no pre-existing hierarchy of authority.

TEAM FORMATION: TUCKMAN'S STAGES

In 1965 the American psychologist Bruce Tuckman laid down what has become a well-known 'model' of this development of a team, giving the four stages of development four rhyming words to define the primary activity in each stage:

1 Forming

In this stage, the group physically comes together, says hello, shakes hands and introduces themselves.

2 Storming

In this stage, the individuals in the group start to 'suss each other out':

- who is quiet
- who will take on tasks without complaint
- who will always want to be heard
- who has natural authority

- who had 'good' ideas
- who is cautious
- who is a risk-taker
- who wants to talk and who wants to act
- who has specialist skill or knowledge that can be of help
- who is the best leader.

During this stage there will also be unstructured debate regarding:

- *What is it that we are trying to achieve?* (This may seem obvious but it is often less clear than you might think; for instance, are we trying to stay alive and stay put for the rescuers to find us, or are we trying to walk out of the desert and reach safety ourselves?)

- *How are we going to achieve it – what is the plan?* Do we head north, east, south or west? Do we put all our efforts into saving the injured who cannot save themselves, or do we leave them and save those with the greatest chance of survival?

This could take a matter of minutes or a matter of days. It could be cyclic: the group may adopt a structure and a plan only to reject it later, usually in the face of a mishap or setback.

3 Norming

Eventually, the natural followers will begin to follow and the natural leaders will begin to lead, some sort of consensus will be achieved (or at least appear to be achieved) and the group will start to act as a team.

4 Performing

Now everyone knows what they are supposed to be doing and who to turn to when they need support and decisions. Now the team is performing.

COACHING SESSION 35

Tuckman's stages and you

How might Tuckman's ideas about team formation be related to good management practice?

Write down your ideas here.

_____

_____

_____

_____

_____

_____

_____

_____

_____

_____

_____

BUILDING A TEAM

We've looked at this in the situation of a totally random group make-up, so what has that got to do with being a manager and managing a work team? The answer is quite simple. You probably didn't select every member of the team who works for you, you probably inherited some of them. You may have had some of them foisted upon you by your boss, and some of these will be great. Some may be there because they have failed elsewhere and the organization's other managers didn't have the gumption to sack them. Some of them may be temporary, such as graduate trainees who will be with you for just a couple of months. Or your whole team may be allocated full- or part-time to work together temporarily on a specific project that you are managing, again full- or part-time.

As a manager, you want your team to go from forming to performing as quickly as possible; you don't want to wait and let it happen naturally and by default. It will happen by default – it is human nature. Look back at Chapter 3 on managing your own motivation, and you will see that the third level in Maslow's Hierarchy of Needs is a 'sense of belonging to a team, tribe, gang or family'. Ninety-nine per cent of people want to belong to a team, they like being with like-minded people and having that sense of security and belonging. Your challenge is to make them want to belong to *your* team.

So the fundamental questions are:

- Do your team members feel that they are actually part of your team?
- Are they satisfied with the way the team operates?

Of course, if you ask those questions directly, you are unlikely to get an honest answer. So Coaching session 36 is a suggested process for getting a team together and taking it to the performing state as quickly and sensibly as possible.

ONLINE RESOURCE

Facilitator guide: team-building

To help you to run the team-building meeting outlined below, there is a downloadable 'Facilitator guide' at:

www.TYCoachbooks.com/Management

COACHING SESSION 36

An agenda for team-building

Contact all the team members and give them notice that you are going to hold a team-building session at a suggested time and place for a couple of hours.

Send out an agenda for the event in advance, asking people to give some thought to the content and their contribution to it. The agenda might look something like this:

Agenda		
Item	Objective	Timing
What are we here for?	To investigate and clarify the objective of the team as a whole	15 minutes
Knowing me, knowing you	To get to know each other on a more personal basis than job roles; please prepare a three-minute introduction about yourself your role and responsibilities. Include one wish that you have relating to the behaviours within the team.	number of team members × 3 minutes

Team charter	To create a commonly accepted 'charter' of acceptable behaviours within the team to make it easier for all to focus on the task rather than interactions and conflicts	45 minutes to 60 minutes
Team Name	To create a snappy and accepted name for our team that we can use among ourselves and to the wider world	25 minutes
Thanks and close	Thank everyone	

Once you have done this, write up some notes about how it went – what went well, what went not so well and how would you do it differently in the future.

What went well

_____

_____

_____

_____

_____

_____

_____

_____

What went not so well

_____

_____

_____

_____

_____

_____

_____

_____

_____

What you would do differently next time

_____

_____

_____

_____

_____

_____

_____

_____

MAINTAINING A TEAM

Once a team is in performing state, there is a tendency to allow focus on the actual teamworking to drift and to focus solely on the results, outputs and achievements of the team. This is wholly natural and not unreasonable, except that it means that the first indicator that things are going wrong tends to be when the team starts to fail to achieve its goals. If you wait until the team is failing before trying to get the teamworking right again, you are shutting the metaphorical stable door after the horse has bolted. Consequently, it is a good idea to keep your finger on the pulse of the team working regardless of whether the team is hitting its targets or not. There are two ways that you can do this:

1. **Covertly** – by simply watching and listening to the team members as they go about their day-to-day business. Are they happy and smiling, or are there periods when people are morose and sullen? How often does conversation stop when you or another particular member of the team walks in? Are there unexpected cliques forming either among people of a similar level of experience and authority or among people in similar roles? Are you faced with a constant stream of 'I can't say anything to his/her face but...' types of conversation?

2. **Overtly** – by regularly and frequently getting each member of the team to complete a short assessment of their perceptions of the team working.

If your team is scattered across the organization rather than being located all in one open-plan office, the second option may be the best (or only) way to do this. If you are able to meet people face to face or via a good-quality video link, the sorts of questions you need to ask people are given in Coaching session 37.

COACHING SESSION 37

Maintaining team spirit: a useful questionnaire

Try completing the following questionnaire with your team members. You may have questions of your own to add, so please feel free.

To what degree do people put the interests and priorities of the team ahead of the interests and priorities of their respective jobs or functions?

How well do we obtain, provide and use all the needed information and assistance from each other when solving problems or making decisions?

How well organized and structured are we for the tasks we have to perform?

How good are our problem-solving processes and methods?

How good are our decision-making processes and methods?

How effective am I at providing the direction, guidance and resources the team needs?

To what extent do people express their opinions honestly and openly to one other?

How good are we at using the time we spend together productively?

How much do we all know about what other team members expect from us?

How good are we at surfacing and managing disagreements between us in a constructive way?

ONLINE RESOURCE

Maintaining team spirit in a remote team: questionnaire

If you are based in different countries and can't do this face to face, then give serious consideration to doing this by using a survey. Download a questionnaire that you can mail out to people.

www.TYCoachbooks.com/Management

→ NEXT STEPS

In this chapter we have looked how teams develop naturally and how you, as a team manager, can aid and smooth this process. In the coaching sessions you were encouraged to engage in team-building activities and to maintain a team's effectiveness through an ongoing assessment of its 'health'.

In the next chapter we focus on another key ingredient in managing a 'healthy' team – your team members' development and performance. This is a long and tough chapter, so do set plenty of time aside to work your way through it.

TAKEAWAYS

How good do you think you are at building and maintaining your team?

_____

_____

_____

_____

_____

_____

_____

_____

_____

_____

How will you change the way you build teams in the future?

_____

_____

_____

_____

_____

_____

_____

_____

_____

_____

_____

How will you change the way you maintain teams in the future?

_____

_____

_____

_____

_____

_____

_____

_____

MANAGING YOUR TEAM MEMBERS' DEVELOPMENT AND PERFORMANCE

11

 OUTCOMES FROM THIS CHAPTER

- Understand the value of managing your team members' development effectively, in terms of the individual, the team and the organization.

- Learn how to manage team members' performance on an ongoing basis, not just once a year!

- Acquire some simple procedures for responding to team members' performance, both good and bad.

'Sustainability' is a buzzword of the twenty-first century. We want sustainable energy, products from sustainable sources and sustainable government policies. As managers, we also want sustainable teams. This means that we need to be developing our people for tomorrow and the next day as well as managing their performance today.

MANAGING DEVELOPMENT

Most of us have an annual appraisal with our boss, and this usually includes a section on development (though this is often referred to as 'training needs'). The sad reality is that many people find that, if they have the meeting in March, the forms are filed away and only pulled again the next February and dusted off for the next appraisal. At that point, someone realizes that no action has been taken in terms of the identified development needs (usually a training course booking) and it is now too late to actually get it scheduled this year. It is added to next year's 'plans'. Anecdotal evidence has suggested that some items on such appraisals have been carried over for as long as eight years before they finally get dropped.

Though most managers have a formal responsibility for developing their staff, very few managers who fail to do so (or fail to do so effectively) suffer any detriment to their career for this failing. This is why the management of people's development is so often so poorly done.

COACHING SESSION 38

Do you develop your team members?

Try to answer these question as honestly as you can. If you are failing in this respect, you are certainly not alone.

Do you have a frequent and regular review of the planned development needs of your team?

_____

_____

_____

_____

_____

How often during the year do you add specific development plans for people?

_____

_____

_____

_____

_____

_____

There are three areas, or guides, for assessing people's developmental needs – the organizational needs, the team needs and individuals' needs.

1 The organizational needs

Do you plan development of the individual in relation to the organization – changes in work practices, software/machinery, products and services, internal policies, industry-wide legislation, and so on? In these instances, all the members of the team may have identical needs.

'Machinery' includes not just big pieces of specialist equipment but everyday things such as an updated software package or even a new desk phone (do people know how to transfer calls, set and pick up VM remotely, divert calls to a colleague when out of the office?). One small company I know replaced their desk phones and for three months utter mayhem ensued as calls were lost, callers were left on hold, and voicemail messages went missing. Finally, a series of half-hour sessions were held over a period of a week where people had the new system explained and were given a credit-card-sized reminder and a three-sided desk memory-jogger. Within days, the system was being used to something akin to its full potential.

COACHING SESSION 39

Organization needs

What do you do to plan development of the individual in relation to the organization?

_____

_____

_____

_____

_____

_____

_____

_____

_____

_____

2 The team needs

Do you plan development of the individual in relation to the team: most definitions of a team mention 'complementary skills' (see Chapter 7). This means that the development needs of one member of the team may need to take into account the skills and abilities of the other team members, not just in their specialist technical knowledge, though this is clearly important, but also in their personal skills. For instance, if you already have a team member who is a good 'door-opener' with regard to selling, you may now need a person who is a good 'wing-man'. Whereas, if you have already got two good 'account managers' in the team but no proactive salespeople, you really need a good door-opener, and another account manager would be more detrimental than helpful. If you already have a person who is great at generating creative ideas, you might need a person who is better at the 'nuts and bolts' of making the creative idea into a reality.

COACHING SESSION 40

Team needs

How balanced are your team's skills? What are you missing or, even, what do you have too much of?

_____

_____

_____

_____

_____

_____

_____

_____

How could improve this state of affairs?

_____

_____

_____

_____

_____

_____

_____

_____

3 The individuals' needs

Do you plan development of an individual with relation to their current job role needs?

Clearly, someone needs to have the skills to fulfil the job they currently do. This will include their personal skills and knowledge as well as their technical skills and knowledge. For instance, a team member may be an excellent 'accounts assistant' with a first-class knowledge of spreadsheet set-up, data entry, trial reconciliations and double-entry bookkeeping, but they may lack the communication skills for the credit-control aspects of their role.

Do you realistically plan development of an individual in relation to the next step on their career ladder? This is critical for people's motivation as it permanently reminds them that you are rooting for their long-term life rather than just squeezing every last drop of productivity out of them today. For this topic, timing is the most important issue: if a person is fully skilled for promotion but there is no substantive role for them to step into for a year, they will become demotivated and will lose the skills they learned through lack of practice. If they are promoted to the role before they are fully skilled for it, there is an increased chance of one of two things happening:

1. They will fail in their new job and be deemed to have reached 'their level of incompetence'.

2. They may well learn bad habits before anyone sets up a suitable learning opportunity for them.

 COACH'S TIP

The Peter Principle

According to the Peter Principle, people are promoted up to their level of incompetence and then their career stops. The theory goes that we are promoted because we excel at today's job and no one can tell that we don't have the ability to do the job one level higher. Only by being given that role do we prove that we can't do it but by then there is too much 'face' at stake to reduce the person in rank back to their level of competence. This explains why so many managers manage to make so much of a mess of so much of their job!

In either case, after a short while, attending any sort of learning opportunity, be it a training course, the intervention of a coach or even distance learning or reading, is deemed inappropriate. To be seen to do so would be an admission of failure (either on the part of the individual concerned or the judgement of the person/organization that put them in the role). Consequently, they just continue to bumble along until they retire or quit through 'natural wastage'.

COACHING SESSION 41

Individuals' needs

How do you realistically plan development of an individual in relation to the next step on their career ladder?

_____

_____

_____

_____

_____

_____

_____

_____

_____

_____

_____

_____

_____

_____

_____

_____

_____

_____

COACH'S TIP

A word on training

Training' is not a silver bullet; it is not the solution to all developmental or performance problems.

MANAGING INDIVIDUAL PERFORMANCE

COACHING SESSION 42

Case study: dead wood

Read through the following case study:

A particular company was facing a difficult time in the marketplace and the decision had been taken by the Board that the company's only real chance of weathering the storm was to look to cut its wages bill by 10 per cent. To do this, the decision was made to look to make 10 per cent of the staff redundant.

Senior management wanted to give the line managers the authority to select the individuals to be let go and so a management meeting was called. An outplacement service was approached and a consultant was asked to join the meeting to handle any ad hoc questions about the support to be offered to the 'unlucky' 1 in 10.

The MD explained the situation to the assembled managers and team leaders, and the HR director explained the process; each manager would rate each of his or her staff against a set of criteria. The 10 per cent of people with the lowest score in their department would be declared redundant. 'This was an opportunity to the long-established company to clear out the dead wood,' as it was put at the meeting.

One manager raised his hand to ask a question of the HR Director, "What if I think that more than 10 per cent of my department is dead wood – can I nominate more than 10 per cent to be made redundant?" At this point, the outplacement consultant asked the HR Director if he could answer the question, which the HR Director allowed him to do. The consultant fixed the individual with a stern look and said: "Only if you put your name at the top of the list, because if you have been responsible for a team and you genuinely believe that more than 10 per cent are dead wood, then you are the deadest wood in the forest.'

The room fell silent for a moment until another manager at the back was heard to whisper, 'Good point!'

Write down your reactions to this case study. Do you, for example, think the consultant was fair in his assessment of the manager?

_____

_____

_____

_____

_____

_____

_____

_____

_____

_____

_____

_____

_____

_____

_____

_____

_____

Managing performance is not just about managing people who are performing badly, it is about:

- Managing people's performance when they are doing a great job, to keep them motivated and ensure that they know that this is what 'great looks like'.

- Managing their performance when they are doing a good job, to help them to recognize that they are appreciated and to help them to raise their game to 'great'.

- Managing their performance when they are doing an OK job, so they know that you have noticed that they aren't doing well and they know that OK isn't good enough and they have the chance to raise their game to 'good' or 'great'.

- Managing their performance when they are doing a lousy job, so you can help them to protect themselves from harsh realities.

- Managing their departure from the team if they are consistent poor performers before their poor performance infects or demotivates the rest of the team.

So everyone in the team needs to be performance-managed, regularly and frequently, for the benefit, not only of the targets and your reputation with your boss, but for their own benefit and the benefit of the rest of the team as well.

COACHING SESSION 43

Self-assessment: managing individuals' performance

How are you doing at managing individuals' performance at the moment? Use the following self-assessment to help you find out.

	Action	Last completed...			
		Yesterday	Last week	Last Month	In the last six months plus
1	Allocation of stretching but equitable targets and objectives with each team member				
2	Catching each person doing things right and giving them a verbal token of appreciation (e.g. a 'thank you')				
3	Seeing someone behaving in an unacceptable way and addressing the issue in short order (within a day or so at a maximum)				
4	Giving someone a bit of praise to their face for a job well done				
5	Reminding someone how their performance and achievement of their objectives affects the team or organization as a whole.				
6	Asking someone how you can help them to perform better				

Assessing your results

- **Action 1**   You really should have done this in the last month or more recently; if you don't do this regularly, people will probably forget what they are supposed to be trying to do!

- **Action 2**   If you are answering these questions on the first day of the working week, then the answer 'last week' is OK. Otherwise, you should have done this yesterday; if you haven't, there are really only two possible reasons:

1. Every member of your team is completely useless (in which case, you are failing abysmally as a manager; see 'Six of the Best' later in this chapter); *or*

2. You are behaving like an ungrateful manager, which is not motivating for people.

■ **Action 3**   It depends. If no one in your team has actually behaved in a way which is unacceptable, then you are a probably already a very good team manager. Alternatively, it could be that you are not spending enough 'face time' with the team to see what actually goes on day to day. Or it could be that you set very low standards and accept almost any behaviour!

■ **Action 4**   If you are answering these questions on the first day of the working week, then the answer 'last week' is OK. Otherwise, you should have done this yesterday. If you haven't, there are really only two possible reasons:

1. No one in your team is actually doing anything right (in which case, you are failing abysmally as a manager; see '7-Up' later in this chapter); *or*

2. You are behaving like a manager who doesn't even recognize good work and effort, which is not motivating for people.

■ **Action 5**   'When you are up to your a** in alligators it is often easy to forget that the initial objective was to drain the swamp.' Many people's day-to-day jobs can seem pretty pointless when viewed out of context. However, you are digging that ditch...

- to drain the water,

- to dry out the land

- and clear the swamp

- to destroy the habitat and breeding grounds of the mosquitoes

- that carry the malaria that kills 1.2 million people a year.

Put like that, digging a ditch suddenly goes from being back-breaking, boring and unskilled work of apparently little value to being a back-breaking, boring job that is just as critical in saving 1.2 million lives per annum as being the Professor of Tropical Medicine at the World Health Organization.

Consequently, you should have answered 'yesterday' or 'last week'. If your answer is 'last month', then you may be slipping and presuming that everyone is happy, when they could in fact be beginning to slip into same-old, same-old mode. If your answer was 'in the last six months plus', you really need to get out and do it now!

■ **Action 6.**   The only constant is change; there is always an opportunity to help someone perform 'better' because better could be quicker, less painfully, to a higher quality, more cheaply, with a faster turnaround time or, depending on the role and the output, almost any permutation of these different facets. If someone is performing well, then you can look at ways to make their life easier; if someone is performing less well, then 'better' may be about improving their skills or their resources.

FACTORS THAT AFFECT A PERSON'S PERFORMANCE

There is a wide range of factors that affect a person's performance.

The poet John Donne wrote that 'no man is an island' (take man to mean 'person' here) and it is certainly true that an individual's performance in any field is affected by not only themselves but also external factors.

Consider, if you will, an athlete – a javelin thrower, for example. There are many factors that will affect his or her performance:

- the javelin
- the shoes
- the technique
- the muscle they have
- the wind and light
- the fit of their clothes
- the temperature
- their knowledge of their personal best
- their knowledge of what they are trying to beat
- their will to win
- the actual facilities being used (the terrain etc.)
- how they slept last night
- how they feel this morning
- their desire to please their coach
- the support they feel from the crowd

...and probably some other things as well.

Now, if you consider a different athlete, one who is taking part within a team – say, a relay sprinter – there are other factors that come into play as well:

- the team morale
- the desire to support the team
- the standard of the handover received from the previous runner
- the actual baton: its weight, length and grip-ability.
- the standard of the handover to the next runner
- how much the team has practised together
- the individual's attitude to the other team members
- the competition and how the runner and team are doing in comparison
- the support they feel the other teams are getting from the crowd

...and probably some more as well.

COACHING SESSION 44

Factors that affect performance

Your people will be affected by a similar range of factors: some come from within themselves, some from how they are treated by others and some from the environment in which they find themselves.

Take a few moments to consider what these factors may be:

1. What factors are internal and personal?

_____

_____

_____

_____

_____

_____

_____

_____

_____

_____

_____

2. What factors come from the family?

_____

_____

_____

_____

_____

_____

_____

_____

3. Which come from their relationship with their boss – that is, you?

_____

_____

_____

_____

_____

_____

_____

4. Which come from their co-workers, teammates or colleagues?

_____

_____

_____

_____

_____

_____

5. Which come from customers?

_____

_____

_____

_____

_____

_____

_____

6. Which come from the organization?

_____

_____

_____

_____

_____

_____

_____

_____

7. Which come from the wider environment?

_____

_____

_____

_____

_____

_____

_____

There is a set of 'stock answers' below.

The person themselves. Health, how they are feeling today, personal ambition, personal pride, knowledge, skill, happiness, personal money worries

Their family. Family health and distractions (relationship issues, separation, divorce, sick child, ailing parent); family expectations and drives (desire for a bigger house, higher status, grandchildren, to follow in Dad's/Mum's footsteps, etc.); family time requirements (e.g. school pick-ups and drop-offs)

Their day-to-day relationship with their boss. Desire to please you; desire to aggravate you; whether you've told them off recently; whether you've blamed them/held them responsible for something they perceive as not their fault; clarity of instructions/expectations; whether you're seen as fair or as a pushover. Can they get away with things? Do they think you keep things from them? Do you stand up for them? Do you steal their credit or give it to someone else? Do you smile or scowl? How much responsibility do you give them? Are you approachable? Can they come to you with problems (work/personal)? Do you say thanks and well done? Do you listen? Do you care?

Their relationship with the people they work with. Team spirit, feeling of pride in the team, competitive spirit, co-operative spirit. Do they get back from the team as well as give? Do they like their workmates? Are their workmates 'glass half full' or 'glass half empty' people? Do people talk behind backs?

The customers. Know-alls, militant consumers, unreasonable demands, nice people, smile appreciation/thank you, constant complaints

The organization. Quality of product, quality of support resources (tools, data, supply, etc.); working environment; pay packet; quality of communication with them (are they just a number?); quality of corporate image (are they proud to work for the organization or not?)

The wider environment. The weather, the economy, the media, the government's policies and their perceived effect now and in the future. The individual's spiritual leaders.

How did you do?

! COACH'S TIP

A performance equation

If all these factors affect an individual performance, we can probably accept the 'equation':

$$\text{Performance} = \frac{\text{Skill} + \text{Will}}{\text{Environment}}$$

This is a valuable equation for one primary reason: if you don't accurately diagnose the cause of poor performance, you will probably prescribe a treatment that is ineffective.

COACHING SESSION 45

Case study

Read the following case study:

A manager had spent his entire corporate life with the commercial arm of a high-street bank. His role was to manage business accounts in the local area and his portfolio stretched from one-man bands to multi-million-pound businesses.

Every year for the past 12 years he had been successful in all aspects of his role bar one – he had never hit the sales target set for the generation of revenue through business insurances.

Every year he had had an annual appraisal with his boss and every year, as a result of this performance failure, his boss had sent him on the training course for selling insurance products. The course was generally seen as a good course; it was updated each year to reflect the changing products, legislation, customer needs and corporate image. Every year the manager spent three days on the course and every year he passed the assessment with flying colours. But he never hit the target; in spite of the target clearly being perfectly achievable.

What would your diagnosis of this poor performance be?

_____

_____

_____

_____

_____

_____

_____

_____

_____

_____

_____

_____

_____

_____

_____

_____

The thirteenth year the individual had a conversation with a young graduate who had been trained as a non-directive coach and who understood the performance equation above. Within 20 minutes, it became clear that the problem wasn't a lack of skill, but a rejection of the role of 'insurance salesman' – that is, it was lack of 'will'. Twelve years of three-day training courses were wasted!

TWO TOOLS TO HELP YOU TO MANAGE PEOPLE'S PERFORMANCE

It is easy to know that you should manage people's performance every day, but it is less easy to actually do it. Many managers shy away from 'catching people doing things right' for fear of making people complacent, or they rationalize that doing things right is, after all, is what people are being paid to do.

Similarly, many managers shy away from managing poor performance for fear of upsetting people (particularly if, not so long ago, the manager was one of those people's teammates). The increasing, and increasingly complex, laws relating to bullying and harassment, unfair discrimination and human rights, also contribute to a laissez-faire attitude among many managers.

Here are two simple and practical tools to help you manage people's performance on a day-to-day basis.

'Six of the Best'

This is a quick and easy process to follow (experience shows that it usually takes about two minutes) when you catch someone doing something right. It is called 'Six...' because there are six steps and it is called '...of the Best' because it is about good performance.

1. **Identify and describe the good performance** Don't be ambiguous, nail your colours to the mast in terms of your opinion. For instance, 'Pat, this report you have written regarding the benefits of changing to Microsoft Outcast – it's really good. It is succinct, to the point and quantified in terms of money savings and time savings. Well done!'

2. **Ask the person how they feel about it.** The idea here is to get them to verbalize how good they feel.

3. **Ask what parts went particularly well and why.** This is to get them to reflect on the specific things that they did that contributed to the success. (Remember experiential learning and the value of reflection to learn from past successes and failures! See Chapter 5.)

4. **Summarize the reasons for success.** This is your chance to demonstrate that you listened to them and value the things they did. Here you can add any other factors that contributed such as a teammate's support or a good resource. The objective here is for you to tell them the things to repeat in order to repeat the success. This is reinforcement.

5. **Ask what they would do differently next time.** The objective here is to get them to look at things to change to make it even better. It is a subtle way of getting them to reflect on the things that they did but would not do again, or the things that they didn't do but would do next time.

6. **Ask what they have learned from this.** Here you are looking for a summary of all the learning aspects, with the additional aim of underlining the fact that they can and do succeed and that you notice!

'7-Up'

This is another quick and easy process, this time to use when you catch someone performing poorly. They could be failing to hit a goal or target or exhibiting a simple behaviour that is not acceptable (it could be something that is against best practice, corporate procedure or the team charter). It is called '7' due to the seven steps and 'up' because it refers to its aim of raising the poor performance. It isn't just a question of a reprimand or a warning; it is a process to identify causes of poor performance and ways to improve.

1. **Outline the poor performance.** Don't beat around the bush or be 'mealy-mouthed';' nail your colours to the mast with a short statement that relates solely to the poor performance observed. For instance: 'Pat, that customer clearly felt that you were being rude; she had a face like thunder and she simply turned her back and walked straight out of the shop.'

2. **State the impact on the individual and team.** The objective here is to highlight the importance of the matter. A lost customer is lost revenue; errors have to be rectified, and so on. Simply telling someone that lateness, for instance, is a breach of contract seldom has any effect, so try to avoid 'the letter of the law' argument at all times.

3. **Ask their point of view.** This is your chance to show that you are being fair by listening to their point of view, their reasons, rationale and/or excuses. Here is where you make the judgement as to whether the performance failure was down to skill, will or environment. Use this equation to test and probe whether they are giving you an answer which you think is 'glib'. So if Pat's 'justification' for being rude to the customer is that he/she was not feeling well (environment), ask whether they know that being rude to a customer is never a good idea. If the answer to that is 'yes', then the failure was caused by a lack of will. Pat knew it was wrong but did it anyway. At this stage, constrain yourself to asking questions – don't issue judgements or offer solutions.

4. **Ask what they can do to improve.** The objective here is to get the person to identify their own solutions to the problem. If you do it for them, they have no vested interest in making the solution work, and if it fails, it was your plan so you are a bad manager. Keep them on the matter of what *they* can do.

5. **Ask what help they need from others.** Here is your chance to show that you want to take all measures to help them to improve. 'Help' in this instance could be provision of extra resources or support from another person to show/train/coach. It could be a consistent reminder from others to the person concerned. It could be a training course.

6. **Get them to summarize the plan that arises from the above.** Again, the objective is to get them to verbalize the plan for improvement. This increases their understanding and ownership of their own performance.

7. **Ask the qualifying/committing question.** This is your gift of a 'last chance' at getting it right. For instance, 'So, Chris, if you do the things you have outlined and I provide you with the support you have asked for, can you assure me that this won't happen again?' Then wait for a definite answer. If the person has any other, hitherto hidden, causes for failing, this is the point at which they are most likely to lay them out on the table. It will be annoying to have got this far without knowing the full picture but at least you now have the chance to put a realistic solution in place. If you don't, the consequence is likely to be a repeat of this conversation in a few days, weeks or months. Imagine if the bank manager's manager in Coaching session 45 had asked this question; then it is likely that 12 years of consistent failure could have been avoided and a great deal of money could have been saved.

ONLINE RESOURCE

An aide-memoire

You can download an a printable desk-reminder of the 'Six of the Best' and the '7-Up' processes. Lots of managers find it really helpful to have this to hand as an aide-memoire.

www.TYCoachbooks.com/Management

COACHING SESSION 46

Test your reactions

Look at the following scenarios. What would be your reaction as the manager?

Test 1

You asked a member of your team to carry out a feasibility study on a new piece of equipment. They have produced the report which is excellent in its assessment of the usability of the equipment, the compatibility with current processes and the service backup. The only thing missing is any mention of the cost or any cost–benefit analysis.

What would you do now?

_____

_____

_____

_____

_____

_____

_____

_____

_____

_____

Test 2

You have just overheard one of your most experienced and successful members of staff chatting to a new person in the team while having a cigarette outside the building. The old hand is describing a customer in derogatory and sexist terms.

What would you do now?

_____

_____

_____

_____

_____

_____

_____

Test 3

One of your team has come to you and 'confessed' that they have _just_ made a relatively serious mistake; they have accidentally mailed out an invoice to a customer for a significant bill that should have gone to another customer. Unfortunately, the customer concerned had a complaint only last week which you have just managed to sort out.

What would you do now?

_____

_____

_____

_____

_____

_____

_____

_____

Test 4

A member of your team has come in to work 45 minutes late. They look terrible and have gone straight to their workstation and sat down and started to work. They haven't spoken to you or anyone else about their lateness – not to explain or to apologize.

What would you do now?

_____

_____

_____

_____

_____

_____

_____

_____

_____

Test 1

This is a perfect scenario to use 'Six of the Best'. You are pleased with the overall good performance and you can guide the individual to see the way to make a good report even better by adding the cost–benefit element of feasibility.

Test 2

In this instance, you really must carry out a '7-U' with the experienced member of staff. Obviously, do this in private if at all possible. They may be a good performer generally, but this is behaviour which is unprofessional and possibly contrary to the law as well. When explaining the impact, although you could mention the legal aspects (or company policy issue), you should emphasize the potentially damaging aspect of holding derogatory opinions of customers and of sharing them with others, especially someone potentially easily led such as a new starter.

You will probably also benefit from taking the new starter to one side and clearly explaining that such opinions are not acceptable and that you have had words with the person who was voicing them.

Test 3

This is actually two straightforward situations; 1) you need to do a 'Six of the Best' with the team member for their recognition that they have made a mistake **and** their honesty in being open about it immediately. Then 2) you need to carry out a '7-Up' about the cause of the problem and the action to take to prevent it happening again.

Then, of course, you go into problem-solving mode to actually manage the situation (or get the team member to manage the situation).

Test 4

You must go down the route of a '7-Up'. Regardless of the reasons that may come out in stage 3, the fact that they are late **and** have not given any warning or apology is unacceptable. It may come out that they have been drinking the night before, or that they had been in A&E all night with their partner, or they have just been diagnosed with cancer. The answer you get in stage 3 will dictate what your reaction is thereafter but you still have a responsibility to get to that point by covering stages 1 and 2.

→ NEXT STEPS

In this chapter we have tackled how you manage your team's development and performance. These are aspects that are often neglected by managers, even those who show excellence in other aspects of their work, but they are nonetheless vital to successful management. Observing, assessing and, where necessary, intervening to ensure a good or even great level of performance will help you, your team members and your organization flourish.

In Chapter 12, we look at a special case – how to manage a team remotely.

 **TAKEAWAYS**

How comfortable are you with the development and performance aspects of management? Is there room for improvement?

_____

_____

_____

_____

_____

_____

_____

_____

_____

_____

How will you change the way you manage your team members' development after reading this chapter?

_____

_____

_____

_____

_____

_____

_____

_____

_____

_____

_____

How will you change the way you manage your team members' performance after reading this chapter?

_____

_____

_____

_____

_____

_____

_____

_____

_____

_____

_____

_____

_____

_____

_____

_____

MANAGING A REMOTE TEAM

12

 OUTCOMES FROM THIS CHAPTER

- Understand the particular requirements of managing a remote/virtual team.
- Draw up a communications management plan for a remote/virtual team.
- Consider appropriate communications technologies for managing a remote/virtual team.
- Learn how to maximize the team spirit of a remote/virtual team.

Everything we have covered so far about managing your team and managing people's performance has presumed that you work in an environment where you and your team are co-located for either all or most of the time. When a team is scattered across the country or the globe, there are some added issues:

- It is harder for each person to know what everyone else is doing; this can lead to feelings of isolation and also to duplication of effort.

- It is harder for the team and its goal to remain in clear focus. What tends to be more visible is the immediate geographical environment and the issues therein. This is particularly true when a team member is not only remote from the rest of the team, but is also only a part-time or even casual member of the team. In this instance, he/she has an immediate line manager who is not of the team and teammates and objectives that may clash with the team's objectives.

- Much of the power of each communication is lost through the loss of visual clues of non-verbal behaviours, distortion of voice tone and volume, and, where communication is in writing, the potential for the reader to read it in a way the writer didn't intend (for example, you might read the phrase 'your report was so good' as a sarcastic comment rather than as a statement of praise).

- The physical distance and less frequent communication are apt to make people less caring and considerate of their teammates... Out of sight, out of mind.

- Whereas co-located people will talk to one other by default, the effort of typing an email or text, or dialling the number on the phone, is often seen as disproportionate for merely sociable exchanges. For example, if you entered the office and one of your team was present, you would probably say 'hi' – but would you actually send a text to just say 'hi' to the same teammate if he/she were four hundred miles away?

- Leading on from these things, remote team members in need of support are often reluctant to arrange a conference call or send a request if it is just about the only communication they ever have with you.

The last point is reminiscent of the old joke:

> A young man joins a holy order where the members take a vow of silence. At the end of the first year the Abbot calls the young man to his cell and tells him that he may speak up to five words to the Abbot. The young man thinks about it and then says: 'Beds uncomfortable and food awful.' At the end of the second year the same thing happens, only this time the young man is prepared and, without taking time to reflect, he says: 'Work too hard, no conversation.' At the end of the third year the young man walks into the Abbot's cell and without any preamble says: 'Abbot unhelpful, so I quit.' To which the Abbot replies: 'I'm not surprised – you've been here three years and all you've done since you got here is whinge!'

Some industries have been using remote teams for many years. What follows – the 'Seven good habits of highly effective distance managers' – is the distillation of years of effective management of remote or distance teams, be they full-time teams or matrix teams working on specific projects.

1 DEVELOP AND USE A COMMUNICATIONS MANAGEMENT PLAN

A communications management plan will improve the understanding of the interactions and help to set clear expectations. The communications management plan outlines:

- what formal communication needs to take place
- who needs to be communicated with
- how frequently
- the intention of the communication
- where it originates
- the communication medium
- the actual timing of communication (to take into account people in different time zones)
- the protocol for 'informal' communications (time of day, 'all inform' or one-to-one, 'txt spk' or proper language... What language? Use of emoticons (;-) ☺ ☹), abbreviations and TLAs (three-letter acronyms)

A good remote team manager should take into account (i.e. consult with) the preferences of their team members, but in the end will take responsibility for the plan's ground rules

Once the plan is produced, make it work and keep it 'alive' by amending it in the light of experience and new communication technologies.

COACHING SESSION 47

Develop a communications management plan

Sketch out, in note form, your own communications management plan here.

_____

_____

_____

_____

_____

_____

_____

_____

_____

_____

_____

_____

_____

2 DEVELOP AND USE TEAM GROUND RULES

Ground rules clearly set out the acceptable behaviours among members of the team (including you as the team leader). Depending on the circumstances, they may also set out acceptable behaviours to other 'stakeholders', internal departments, team members' in-country colleagues, and so on.

It is better that the team members create the ground rules themselves rather than you imposing the rules upon them. This ensures that people commit to the ground rules and know that they are fair. This may seem counter-intuitive – you are, after all, supposed to be the leader – but you can lead the team to produce its own rules.

ONLINE RESOURCE

Facilator guide: establishing ground rules

To help you facilitate the team members in drawing up the ground rules, there is a downloadable 'Facilitator guide' at:

www.TYCoachbooks.com/Management

3 SLOW DOWN TO SPEED UP

Slowing down, in practical terms, means to take the time and make the effort to set expectations, to focus, to ensure clarity before plunging into action.

This is a two-way process: For example: the manager knows what the new goals and objectives are and the parameters in which they must be fulfilled. The manager is responsible for ensuring that the team member concerned (the one to whom the responsibility is delegated) is completely clear on the expectations. That team member is now responsible for ensuring that he/she is genuinely and completely aware of the expectations, and also for informing the manager of any potential issues that may affect his or her ability to fulfil those expectations. If one of those issues is their workload from their in-country colleagues, then the manager may have responsibility for helping to smooth those issues directly with the team member's other manager or at a higher level of authority.

It is also the manager's responsibility to ensure that other members of the virtual team are aware of the delegated responsibility, not only where it may impact directly on them, but also for the purpose of furthering a sense of team spirit by simply knowing what others are doing.

This takes time and effort ('slow down') but it will make things quicker and less painful in the long run ('speed up').

4 SELECT APPROPRIATE TECHNOLOGIES FOR TEAM INTERACTIONS

Co-located teams:

- meet formally
- 'chat' informally
- see what each other is doing (in terms of progress)
- see the look on each other's face as they do it (and can see their 'body language')
- see the look on each other's face as they discuss (and can see their 'body language')
- hear the tone of voice that people use when they are talking to each other.

For virtual teams, technology is the communication medium. The order of consideration for selecting a tool for each team interaction should mimic face-to-face interaction as much as possible – economically possible, technologically possible and with regard to efficient time usage.

The priority hierarchy for a team communication (as a group or on a one-to-one basis) would be:

Face-to-face (be that a formal meeting or an informal meeting)

↓

High-quality video (Google +, SKYPE or video call on a mobile network)

↓

Video (if it's a question of one-way communication, this could be set it up as a recorded video message)

↓

High-quality voice and interactive multimedia (such as WebEx, GoToMeeting, Google Hangouts)

↓

Lower-quality voice (mobile phone call or landline call)

↓

Real-time non-voice dialogue (chat room or online forum)

↓

One-way communication with archiving (email or text message, Twitter, social media update).

COACH'S TIP

The closer approximation to face-to-face discussion that any communication technology is able to achieve, the less potential there is for misunderstandings.

Other criteria for selecting communication tools are:

- archiving, record-keeping
- budget
- speed of medium and urgency of message
- confidentiality
- complexity of message
- importance of message
- need for a response ('need' on the part of both parties in the communication)
- ease of use, and availability to all sites
- time of day or night (on the presumption that people may be at home, asleep, etc.).

Working out some of the parameters in your communications management plan will make things work more smoothly.

COACHING SESSION 48

Select appropriate technologies

What communication tools would be the most appropriate to your team interactions?

_____

_____

_____

_____

_____

_____

_____

_____

_____

_____

5 CREATE A VIRTUAL PERSONALITY AND PRESENCE

'Out of sight and out of mind' is a common human attitude that works against you when trying to manage virtually or remotely. Your challenge is to be visible and present, yet not in such a way that you appear oppressive or untrusting. Creating and maintaining a virtual personality and presence is a best practice for leading a team from a distance. Finding the right balance of how frequently to 'show your face' is a critical aspect and it will be dependent on workloads, crises and the personality of the team member concerned.

For example, if you overdo it, important information may get lost in the mass of communications, or you may give the impression of micromanaging, or of lacking trust or confidence. On a practical level, your people may prefer for you just to leave them alone to get on and do some work! If, on the other hand, you become invisible and are not heard from for weeks, it is easier for a team member to misinterpret this in one of several ways:

- The team member doesn't matter to you (or the organization).
- The work they are doing doesn't matter to you (or the organization).
- You are too busy to be disturbed with anything (short of utter disaster).
- Lines of communication have been broken and they are really out there with no support or help.

In any of these cases, the normal human reaction is to move away from you and towards the people the team member does 'see' regularly. They 'go native' and bond with their in-country colleagues at your expense. This is already an issue when the team member is in your own organization's overseas office. However, when the team member is working on a client site, it can be disastrous for you!

Creating a virtual personality requires upfront planning and a keen sense of knowing yourself:

- knowing how your voice (tone and accent, word choice, clarity, and the ability to articulate) is interpreted.
- knowing how strong your written communication is
- knowing how good you are at delegating
- knowing how willing you are to ask for (and get) feedback.

Look back at the section on managing your personal brand. Much of what you need to consider is there, but with the added considerations of distance.

COACHING SESSION 49

Hone your remote brand

Sketch out here how you would adapt your personal brand for remote team management.

_____

_____

_____

_____

_____

_____

_____

_____

_____

6 BE A GREAT HOST

Managing remotely means more time and thought spent in interactions with your team members. The amount of time spent planning for communications and communicating is generally reported to be at least double that for a co-located team. In addition to the formal meetings, the effective virtual team manager finds ways to mimic the informal and unplanned interactions that a co-located team has – such as catching someone in the hall and chatting. Co-located teams inadvertently use these unplanned interactions as precursors for solving problems and getting work done. While it may seem not possible to plan for the unplanned, it is possible to virtually create informal and unplanned ways that the team can interact on a regularly basis.

You need to create a safe and interesting virtual place where team members want to be and to interact. You need to be interested in team members as well as their outputs, and be curious, polite and concerned for their comfort. You also need to recognize when a team member needs/wants to go and get work done. You should ask good questions, listen to answers, be friendly, approachable and fun.

Here are some examples of how some managers have successfully created informal gathering spots for their remote teams:

- Daily five-minute individual phone calls or video calls with each team member. Thirty minutes a day is all it takes to have a five-minute phone call with six team members. For larger teams, either every other day or connecting to key contacts is suggested.

- Create a virtual water-cooler. Keep an online open communication, such as chat room, open all the time for team members to just hang out in. Declare 'break times', 'lunch', 'game time', 'check-in times', etc.

- Hold a 'virtual office' hour. Be online, have open phone lines, and be available at regular times, daily or weekly.

- Create little regular challenges and competitions. The more relevant to the work the better, of course. Make them educational, interesting and fun.

- Create a proactive professional relationship with each team member. This isn't saying that you must become best friends or even like all the team members. It's about understanding who they are, what their career is about, and how they will be able to help with whatever challenges may arise, now and in the future, in their own area of expertise or country, or someone else's.

COACHING SESSION 50

Create a meeting space

Draw up some ideas for your own informal gathering spot.

_____

_____

_____

_____

_____

_____

_____

_____

7 RUN EFFECTIVE VIRTUAL TEAM MEETINGS

Formal team meetings are a given for co-located teams and they cannot be avoided for the virtual team. Virtual team meetings will need to take place via conference call, SKYPE or a similar VOIP or online meeting tool. Most tips and tools for running effective meetings apply for a team that is scattered across different countries (Figure 11.1).

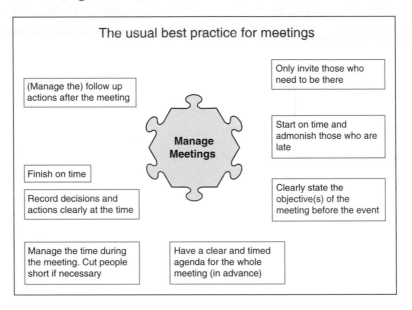

Figure 11.1 The usual best practice for meetings

There are, however, additional practices that apply, and become important, when running virtual team meetings. The virtual team meeting principle is to create, increase and force engagement and interactions from all team members frequently. Here are some techniques that will help in achieving more interaction and engagement on virtual team meetings:

- No long monologues — no one speaks for more than two minutes without interaction from others.

- Ask questions frequently; get answers by a show of hands, a poll or verbally, but get *active* responses.

- Verify and validate that everyone can hear you or another team member when speaking.

- Call on people by names, and get everyone to answer stating their name.

- If possible, use live video on meetings. If not possible (due to bandwidth), have photos of the people so that everyone gets to know their faces as well as their voices.

- Keep track of who spoke on what topic and when.

- Any long explanations should be written down and sent out ahead of time.

- Speak slowly, use short sentences, be concise and avoid slang and cultural references (especially when communicating between people with differing native tongues).

- Make the implicit explicit and describe and state what seems obvious. Examples are: 'We will be closed on Monday for a holiday'; 'A snow storm may cause power outages this week.' These things aren't obvious to people in different countries.

NEXT STEPS

In this chapter we have seen how managing a team remotely or virtually is more challenging than managing a team that is co-located. However, it is entirely doable – it just needs more time and intellectual input from you as a manager. It also poses extra challenges for the team members.

In the next chapter we will turn to a more general theme – motivation.

TAKEAWAYS

If you are the manager of a remote or virtual team, what particular problems do you have?

_____

_____

_____

_____

_____

_____

_____

_____

_____

_____

What do you think are the main differences between managing a co-located team and a remote/virtual one?

_____

_____

_____

_____

_____

_____

_____

_____

_____

_____

_____

How will you change the way you manage remotely after reading this chapter?

_____

_____

_____

_____

_____

_____

_____

_____

MANAGING MOTIVATION

13

✔ OUTCOMES FROM THIS CHAPTER

- Consider and reassess your ideas about your team members' motivation.
- Understand the actual wide range of motivators that keep employees at work.

Back in Chapter 3 we met Maslow's Hierarchy of Needs and discussed your own motivation. As a manager, it is your job to motivate your team. Yes, you can expect a degree of self-motivation from people, but when the chips are down it is up to you to motivate them to work to quality and output standards that are appropriate and acceptable to the organization and commensurate with their salary.

To start with let's do a little diagnosis.

COACHING SESSION 51

Assessment: your team members' motivators

Using the table below, list each of your team members down the left-hand column, and in the middle column all the things that you know, or believe, motivate him or her. In the right-hand column, list the things that you know or suspect will demotivate him or her.

Team member	Motivators?	Demotivators?
E.g. Fred Bloggs	Being left to get on with it, getting a 'thank you' every now and then, and going home at 5.30 on the dot	Team trips to the pub!; senior managers giving awards; me watching over him like a hawk

How much confidence do you have in your answers? If you have lots of confidence, what is it based on? Experience of specific incidents and comments, or a generic 'guess'?

_____

_____

_____

_____

Different organizations have done surveys into staff motivation over the years and, notwithstanding the different types of industries and jobs, they come up with pretty similar results.

In 2008 a survey was carried out in the UK in a nationwide organization. This employed people from both sales and service disciplines, technical and non-technical roles, management positions and administrators. The motivators were ranked by a group of people in excess of 1,200 strong.

Below are the top ten motivators, ranked in order of importance:

1. **The resources they are provided with to do their job.** This covers tools and materials, and also their work environment; the area where they meet with and interact with customers, as well as the 'Staff Only' areas, office, workshop, staffroom and so on.

2. **Their relationship with their immediate manager.** This includes the issue of trust and authority that each person has as an individual to work under their own initiative. Are they treated as intelligent people with brains and a set of ethics, or as if they are untrustworthy idiots who need to be watched all the time?

3. **The way the organization communicates with them.** This covers:

   - Are people expected to read up on stuff in their own time?

   - Are they told in a timely fashion or do they hear about things on the grapevine or even read them in the newspaper?

   - Are people given the whole story, or is much of it deemed to be 'above them' or kept from them on a 'need-to-know' basis?

   - How are messages disseminated in a way that everyone from the office staff to the truck drivers can access?

   - Is the language appropriate to the audience (i.e. not too highfalutin but not dumbed down either)? Communication being a two-way process, this also covers what mechanisms and attitudes exist for people to feed back to management.

   - Are managers accessible to everyone or do the 'gatekeepers' keep hoi polloi out of the walnut corridors of the executive suite?

4. **Team spirit.** This is at various levels. For instance, is there a team spirit among the members of the sales team? Between the sales team and the other teams in sales and marketing? Between sales and marketing and the logistics and manufacturing functions, and between the different offices and between the UK subsidiary and the European parent? (A negative team spirit can also exist between the 'workers' and the 'management'. This may be a motivator but it may well be motivating people in an 'unhelpful' direction!)

5. **Their 'pay' package.** This is not just the salary, but also overtime, bonus, holiday entitlement, pension and any other allowances. It also includes such elements as zero-hours contracts, non-disclosure agreements, non-competition clauses and similar (especially where it seems that these are one-sided – to the benefit of the employer and to the detriment of the individual).

6. **Recognition of their achievements.** This includes everything from a 'thank you' and a 'well done', to a corporate award, a 'puff' in the in-house, trade or local newspaper/website, right up to a recommendation for a medal in the New Year Honours list. It excludes 'compensation and benefits' – that is, the money.

7. **Job security.** Well, at least the perception of it! This is the 'psychological contract' that says that the organization and its managers will look after loyal staff rather than looking solely at the bottom line and where they can find a cheaper pair of hands.

8. **The 'fit' between them and their job.** Do they actually have the personality and the skill to do it happily? Bearing in mind the pace of technological change, this is a big element in people's day-to-day motivation. Also bear in mind that an individual's motivation changes as they become older and take on different life choices. For instance, a youngster with no family ties may relish overseas travel, but five years later, now with a partner and a child, they may be more motivated by stability than excitement.

9. **Training and development opportunities.** Is there a future for them... even if it isn't to become the MD. See below for a discussion about people who appear to have 'no ambition'.

10. **Organizational culture and values.** Do they actually match with the individual's personal values and, perhaps more to the point, are the organizational values actually alive at all levels in the organization?

Over the years studies have also shown that many managers presume that the things that motivate their staff are simply money and more money. Clearly, this is erroneous.

Compare your thoughts in Coaching session 52 with the list above. Does your perception relate to the 'norm'? If it does, great. If not, you should consider spending more time with your people finding out what really motivates them, so that you can ensure that your everyday behaviours balance their needs with the organization's requirements.

COACHING SESSION 52

Your sense of agency

Consider again the top ten motivators. Taking one of your team members as an example, ask yourself how much control you have over each motivator on a scale of 0–10 (with 0 meaning 'no control' and 10 meaning 'complete control. (Remember the discoveries about 'proactivity and a 'sense of agency' in Chapter 3.)

1. The resources they are provided with to do their job	0 1 2 3 4 5 6 7 8 9 10
2. Their relationship with their immediate manager	0 1 2 3 4 5 6 7 8 9 10
3. The way the organization communicates with them	0 1 2 3 4 5 6 7 8 9 10
4. Team spirit	0 1 2 3 4 5 6 7 8 9 10
5. Their 'pay' package	0 1 2 3 4 5 6 7 8 9 10

6. Recognition of their achievements	0 1 2 3 4 5 6 7 8 9 10
7. Job security	0 1 2 3 4 5 6 7 8 9 10
8. The 'fit' between them and their job	0 1 2 3 4 5 6 7 8 9 10
9. Training and development opportunities	0 1 2 3 4 5 6 7 8 9 10
10. Organizational culture and values	0 1 2 3 4 5 6 7 8 9 10

Here are my ideas about the degree of control you have over each of these motivators (feel free to disagree!):

1. *The resources they are provided with to do their job.* As their manager you have either total control over this or at least a large degree of influence over it.

2. *Their relationship with their immediate manager.* This is almost completely within your control.

3. *The way the organization communicates with them.* You have little control over how your bosses communicate downwards, but you have influence; if not told, you can ask.

4. *Team spirit.* This is very much within your sphere of influence; the way you manage will strongly affect the team spirit. Are they with you or in spite of you?

5. *Their 'pay' package.* Though the organization may have strict pay banding, you still have some opportunity to influence what band a person is on.

6. *Recognition of their achievements.* This is totally within your control: you can recognize a person's achievements and you can tell your boss about them.

7. *Job security.* You can't guarantee this but you can fight the good fight for it.

8. *The 'fit' between them and their job.* You can monitor this and help to either mould the job to suit a person (if the person is worth it) or help the person to see that they aren't suited and support them in finding a job that is more appropriate to them.

9. *Training and development opportunities.* This is almost completely within your power. Even if you have no budget you can develop a person's skills and ability, as seen in Chapters 9 and 11.

10. *Organizational culture and values.* You can personally live the organizational values and manage them within your team. This can have a beneficial effect on other people outside your team.

So motivating your team and its individual members is something that is not only vitally important in your job as a manager, but is also something that you have a very high degree of control over.

SOME THOUGHTS ABOUT PEOPLE WHO CLAIM TO HAVE 'NO AMBITION'

Since the collapse of a rigid class structure, the received wisdom in the Western world has been that everyone strives to improve their lot and that of their descendants. That means trying to get promoted. In the postmodern world there are many people who recognize that their immediate quality of life is more important to them than rising up the corporate ladder or gaining the money to buy material things tomorrow. Consequently, many people claim to have 'no ambition'. But do they really have no ambition, or do they simply not subscribe to the definition of ambition that might be summed up as 'onwards and upwards'?

- To be a good parent is an ambition.

- To enjoy your hobbies is an ambition.

- To look after your elderly parents (as opposed to 'to earn enough to be able to afford £6,000 per annum in care-home fees') is an ambition.

- To live in society without claiming benefits is an ambition.

- To do God's work is an ambition.

- To always have enough to eat is an ambition!

😀😀 COACHING SESSION 53

Action plan: motivation

Complete the following table with actions that you will take to either improve, or maintain, the levels of motivation among your team. For each quadrant consider each member of the team and consider each of the top ten motivators.

Things to do more of	Things to start doing

Things to do less of	Things to stop doing

ONLINE RESOURCE

Action plan: motivation (template)

Download a copy of this template to use with multiple team members.

www.TYCoachbooks.com/Management

NEXT STEPS

Managers tend to be cynical when it comes to looking at people's motivation in the workplace. Their own motivation always seems to be so much more high-minded than the motivation of anyone else! In reality, as we have seen in this chapter, employees' motivations are usually much broader than merely a decent salary and an easy life. If a manager were to manage a team on that basis, he/she would soon discover that their cynicism led them up a blind alley. A good manager will recognize a rich range of motivators that will vary from person to person.

In the next chapter we will look at managing other managers' people, by which I mean maximizing your powers of negotiating and influencing across your organization.

👍 TAKEAWAYS

Before you read this chapter, what, broadly, was your stance on your team members' motivation?

_____

_____

_____

_____

_____

_____

_____

_____

_____

Has this now changed?

_____

_____

_____

_____

_____

_____

_____

_____

_____

_____

How will you build on your team members' motivation after reading this chapter?

_____

_____

_____

_____

_____

_____

_____

_____

MANAGING OTHER MANAGERS' PEOPLE

14

OUTCOMES FROM THIS CHAPTER

- Learn how to maximize your negotiating skills.
- Understand how to use the logos–ethos–pathos paradigm to become an effective influencer.

Increasingly, we all work in matrix structures where the old-fashioned ranks and hierarchies are gone. Influencing people rather than giving orders is more the twenty-first-century way. This chapter will help you find ways of influencing effectively to make your life easier.

Managing other managers' people is about 'negotiating' and 'influencing'. You may be negotiating with the manager to get them to give you authority over their staff or you may be negotiating with their staff to reach a mutually acceptable outcome in terms of quality standard, workload or output. The key words here are 'mutually acceptable' – you have to have a solution that is acceptable to you, otherwise you might as well just do the work yourself. They have to have a solution that is acceptable to them because, ultimately, it is their other workload that they are most judged upon.

KNOWING WHAT YOU WANT

When starting a negotiation it is always 'best' to know what you want out of it. You need to consider:

- **Your stance and what you want to gain from the situation**. For example, you want Steph Smith to design a building layout that maximizes user space and minimizes energy consumption, and you need to have the rough design to deliver to the client at a meeting at 11.00 on 5 December (i.e. a SMART objective).

- **Your BATNA.** This is an acronym for 'Best Alternative To a Negotiated Agreement' (Batna is also the name of a town in Algeria, but that is another story).

Depending on the circumstances, a BATNA may have almost any range of constituent parts, but always remember that the BATNA may well be something like: 'I walk away from this negotiation having agreed that we are not going to agree to anything other than not to agree.' For example, in the instance above, your BATNA could range from formally reporting the person for failing to provide support, to contracting an outside agency to produce the design.

Remember:

- BATNAs change as time changes and will be different for situations that appear similar but are affected by deadlines. For example, if the deadline for delivery of the design is in seven weeks, your BATNA may include finding an external subcontractor; if, however, the deadline is tomorrow, then the BATNA may be that you personally will simply burn the midnight oil and do the job yourself, or that you will renegotiate the deadline with the client.

- BATNAs are also usually a full package, not a single issue. For example, If I can't get Steph to do this job, my best alternative will be to go outside and find a subcontractor. If I have to do this, I need to know whether I already have a potential source of subcontractors and whether I have an external budget, and, if so, how much it is.

Many people don't consider their BATNA for two reasons:

1. Denial/preparing to fail: to consider the best alternative to a negotiated agreement is an acceptance that we are likely to fail to reach agreement. This will predispose us to failure.

2. It simply doesn't occur to them.

As you can see, one of the single biggest issues here is actually being in a position to know that you have an alternative. If you don't have at least one (or, at least, you don't feel that you have any alternative), then you will be forced to simply accept the apparent status quo. This is what leads to organizational inertia and that 'Well, that is just how things are done here; there is nothing I can do about it' response to the client when it all fails.

Remember that the BATNA is the best alternative: the best may be to 'go without' or it may be to pay more, accept it later, or lower the quality standard.

You only have to look at an auction to see the potential effects of not considering what constitutes 'best' in advance. People get carried away in the heat of the moment and...

- *either* don't buy something that they really want and need but afterwards realize that the final sale price was well within the bounds of good value for money

- *or* they 'win' the auction and then realize afterwards that they were so desperate to win the lot that they have paid way over the odds (and sometimes way over what they can afford).

COACH'S TIP

Work out your BATNA

When setting out to influence a person over whom you have no solid authority (and we actually live in a free society where even a member of your own team usually has the right to say 'no'), you really need to work out your BATNA.

INFLUENCING

Once you know your BATNA, you need to influence the person to want to do what you want them to do. Here is a strategy which is loosely based on Aristotle's method of proof.

Present to the person a 'balanced' argument which appeals to three different elements:

1 Logos

The Greek word *logos* is the basis for the English word 'logic'. Logos is a broader idea than formal logic, however – logos refers to any attempt to appeal to the intellect, so logos arguments are the ones that focus on the practical and the factual:

- 'Steph, you are simply the only person with the formal qualifications to do this job' is a logos argument.

- 'Steph, you can do this job faster than anyone else', if based in experience, is a logos argument.

- 'Steph, you have time available, whereas everyone else who is capable is up to their eyes on other projects' is a logos argument.

- 'Steph, succeeding in this will give you an extra skill to support your request for promotion' is a logos argument.

COACH'S TIP

WIIFM

Sometimes managers forget the WIIFM factors in their logos arguments; WIIFM stands for 'what's in it for me'. It is sometimes a bit too easy to simply recycle the 'business case' argument when discussing a matter at a more personal level; a cost saving of 4 per cent to the organization may well be the sound business case for something, but does it actually equate to a logical argument for Steph to be doing it?

2 Ethos

Ethos, in this instance, refers to the perceptions of, and relationships with, other people. Ethos is an effective persuasive strategy because we all work with other people and the attitude they have towards us affects our day-to-day motivation. (Remember the top ten motivators – numbers 2, 4 and 6 are directly linked to this element.) For example:

■ 'Steph, doing this will give you the chance to shine in front of one of our most important clients' is an ethos argument.

■ 'Steph, if you take this on it will prove to your teammates just how good you are' is an ethos argument.

■ 'Steph, if you can pull this out of the hat, it will raise your stock no end with your boss and she will see you in a new light' is an ethos argument.

3 Pathos

Pathos elements are about how the individual will feel in themselves about the matter. Obviously, in order to get an effective pathos argument you really need to have a good understanding of the individual you are negotiating with. For instance:

■ 'Steph, think how great you will feel to be up there making this presentation to a really important client' is a pathos argument (as long as you know that you are talking to someone who wants to further their career and will see this as a challenging opportunity rather than a gut-wrenching terror that they would rather avoid at all costs).

■ 'Steph, think how great it will make you feel to be contributing so much to the team' is an pathos argument (as long as you know that Steph actually has some degree of affection and respect for the other members of the team).

Negative arguments

You will notice that all the examples above are 'positive'. You can, of course, use them all in the 'negative' as well:

■ **Negative logos:** 'Steph, if you don't do this for me I'll report you and you will get the sack' is a negative logos argument.

■ **Negative ethos:** 'Steph, if you don't do this, the rest of the team will think that you aren't pulling your weight' is a negative ethos argument.

■ **Negative pathos:** 'Steph, you will kick yourself if you don't do this and then you see someone else getting the kudos' is a negative pathos argument.

As you can imagine, this same balance of arguments can help you to negotiate with the line managers of the people who are in your matrix team.

This strategy helps with people over whom you have no authority, but it is also effective when delegating tasks to people in your own team. It can also work well when managing your boss (see Chapter 15).

COACHING SESSION 54

Reflection

Consider occasions in the past when you have been successful in managing people in matrix situations.

1. What positive logos, pathos and ethos arguments did you use?

_____

_____

_____

_____

_____

_____

_____

_____

_____

_____

2. What negative logos, pathos and ethos arguments did you use?

_____

_____

_____

_____

_____

_____

_____

_____

_____

_____

_____

3. How effective were they? Could you have got the same results with a different approach?

_____

_____

_____

_____

_____

_____

_____

_____

_____

4. What would you do differently if you could replay the time?

_____

_____

_____

_____

_____

_____

_____

_____

_____

NEXT STEPS

In this chapter we have looked at how, as a manager, you can improve your negotiating and influencing skills, both of which are vital in the modern 'matrix' workplace. We have also seen that by understanding and using the logos–ethos–pathos paradigm you can exert a powerful influence on your people, other managers and other managers' people.

In the next chapter we will turn to the topic that often perplexes many managers – how to manage your boss!

👍 TAKEAWAYS

Whom will you make an effort to get to know better so that you can better understand what pathos arguments will be effective? Consider both the individuals and their managers.

_____

_____

_____

_____

_____

_____

_____

_____

_____

What will you seek to understand in order to improve your logos arguments?

_____

_____

_____

_____

_____

_____

_____

_____

_____

_____

How can you improve your understanding of the people whom your 'targets' consider important in order to improve your ethos arguments?

_____

_____

_____

_____

_____

_____

_____

_____

_____

_____

MANAGING YOUR BOSS

15

✔ OUTCOMES FROM THIS CHAPTER

- Use a diagnostic tool to work out what kind of boss you have.
- Learn some simple techniques such as 'High 5' to manage your boss's more negative behaviours.

It is quite possible that your boss is a paragon of management skill and ability and you already feel that he/she needs no management from you. If this is the case you are a) very lucky and b) close to unique! To err is human and so most people find that their boss could use some improvement.

 ### COACHING SESSION 55

Diagnosing your boss

Score your boss 1 to 6, with 1 being 'completely disagree' and 6 being 'agree wholeheartedly'.

Behavioural indicator	Score
My boss welcomes 'phatic' (social) communication with me; says hello and goodbye, smiles.	1 2 3 4 5 6
My boss takes a human interest in my life – health, family, hobbies, weekend, holiday, etc.	1 2 3 4 5 6
My boss is clear what he/she expects of me in terms of my behaviour, outcomes and productivity.	1 2 3 4 5 6
My boss actively asks my opinion of things that relate to my work, such as what support I need, how is my morale, what suggestions do I have.	1 2 3 4 5 6

My boss never criticizes me or my work (or that of co-workers) in front of other people, only in private.	1 2 3 4 5 6
My boss always gives credit where credit is due.	1 2 3 4 5 6
My boss notices when I do things right and frequently says 'thank you' to me for doing my job.	1 2 3 4 5 6
My boss doesn't bear a grudge: if I make a mistake, he/she deals with it and then gets over it and doesn't keep bringing it back up months or years later.	1 2 3 4 5 6
When something goes wrong, my boss is more interested in both helping to put it right and preventing it from recurring, than in allocating blame.	1 2 3 4 5 6
In the event of a customer complaint about something, my boss backs me until or unless it is proven that I have been at fault.	1 2 3 4 5 6
My boss listens to me; both when he/she has asked a question and when I go and speak to him/her.	1 2 3 4 5 6
My boss is completely fair with every person in the team; he/she has no favourite(s).	1 2 3 4 5 6
My boss isn't affected by the latest management 'fad', preferring to stick with sensible and proven ways of motivating and leading us.	1 2 3 4 5 6
My boss doesn't allow any of us to 'coast'; he/she sets challenging, but achievable, targets and makes sure that everyone works hard enough to achieve them.	1 2 3 4 5 6
My boss is genuinely supportive when I or a colleague make a sensible suggestion; he/she never shoots down or buries an idea but always handles it fairly, whether he/she ends up implementing it or not.	1 2 3 4 5 6
Overall totals	**.......out of a possible total of 90**

You have now completed the assessment element of the diagnostic, so now we'll look at the overall scores.

- **If you scored your boss 75–90**, then he/she is a fantastic boss. Rejoice in the fact that, even though you may not have found your career niche, you have certainly found a great person to work for. Copy your boss's behaviours and your people will be grateful and supportive to you. Keep your boss doing the things that he/she is doing and that is all the boss management you need to do.

- **If you scored your boss 60–74**, then you are working for someone who is pretty on-the-ball and, while he/she may not set the world alight, they are certainly in the upper quartile of bosses. You probably don't need to do a lot of managing of this boss, but there may be some areas that you might want to work on depending on the range of scores you have given him/her.

- **If you scored your boss 40–59**, then your boss probably reflects the norm in the developed world: basically competent as a boss for most of the time but sometimes fairly clueless. Remember the equation:

$$\text{Performance} = \frac{\text{Skill} + \text{Will}}{\text{Environment}}$$

It could be that the boss forgets to do some good things or that he/she can't be bothered to make the effort or that he/she has so much on their plate that there just isn't the time. The positive areas, however, give hope for the future and you may well be able to manage your boss to a greater level of ability, so it is still worth sticking with this individual.

- **If you scored your boss 25–39**, then it looks as if you have a boss who exemplifies the 'Peter Principle' (see Chapter 11). He/she has been promoted to their level of incompetence. Probably your boss was a good technician in their previous job and got the promotion in the misguided hope that, by rewarding them, they would somehow metamorphose into a good manager as well. If your boss is still fairly new to management, you may be able to snatch victory from the jaws of defeat; but if he/she is long in the tooth as a manager, then all the bad habits are probably so ingrained that you may be better off devoting your energy to a looking for a new job.

- **If you scored your boss 0–24**, then you really are best advised to not to bother trying to manage your boss at all. He/she is a 'forlorn hope'! Frankly, you are going to have to wait until the boss retires or dies before you get promoted, and it is going to be an unpleasant wait, regardless of how long it takes. So you may be best advised to polish up your CV and get the heck out. Soon... before you pick up some of your boss's nasty habits.

STRATEGIES FOR MANAGING YOUR BOSS

We have two basic strategies here: the first relates to one of the problems that many people face at work and that is how to say 'no'. The second is a methodology that we will relate to the diagnostic that you have just completed. We call it the 'High 5' because it is about looking up and there are five steps.

Saying 'no'

Bosses bring you work to do; if they don't, you could soon be out of a job, but sometimes you can find yourself genuinely with too many tasks for you and your team to successfully achieve in the time available.

Saying 'no' to your boss is sometimes hard; there is an expectation that you will have a 'can do' approach. Your boss may have already given a commitment that the task can be fulfilled. So the difficulty often means that we just keep accepting extra work and tasks and the boss remains blissfully unaware that you and your team are struggling to keep up.

Rather than actually saying 'no', try only giving the rationalization:

> 'Because we are trying to get the exhibition set up we simply can't take on this task as well.'

Or

> 'Because this is coming in so late, we just don't have the time to do it properly before the deadline.'

Alternatively, in order to maintain the 'can do' approach, you could try saying 'yes' but with conditions attached. This helps to communicate the value of the 'yes'. So, for example:

> 'Yes, we can do this for you. Which of our other tasks do you want me not to do?'

or

> 'Yes, we can do that. If you authorize xxx hours overtime in return.'

or

> 'Yes, on this occasion, to help you out, but after today I'm afraid I can't.'

or

> 'Yes, if you can get Alex's team to take over doing Y.'

or

> 'Yes, we can do that for you, but it will have to be next week.'

If you are concerned that your boss will switch off the second they hear the word 'yes', then consider turning the phrasing around. So, for example:

'Yes, we can do this for you, which of my other tasks do you want me not to do?'

would become

'If you can give some of our other tasks to Alex's team, then, yes.'

and

'Yes, we can do that. If you authorize xxx hours overtime in return.'

would become

'If you authorize xxx hours overtime in return, then, yes, I can do that.'

and

'Yes, on this occasion, to help you out, but after today I'm afraid I can't.'

would become

'After today I'm afraid I can't do that but, to help you out, yes, I will on this occasion.'

Sometimes saying 'yes' is a good way to say 'no'. When faced with a 'yes' with conditions, your boss will realize that there are responsibilities both ways.

Continuing the style of 'Six of the Best' and '7-Up' (see Chapter 11), we have a little tool for managing your boss which is called the 'High 5'.

High 5

1. **Explain the behaviour that is presenting a 'problem'.** Get straight to the point, avoid dressing it up or watering it down, and avoid apologizing for it. For instance, 'Alex, you just ticked me off in front of the whole team and in front of customers.'

2. **State the impact of that behaviour.** As with a '7-Up', the objective here is to highlight the importance of the matter. That could be to an individual's morale and productivity, the team or the business as a whole. For instance, 'By doing it in front of everyone you undermine me and make the rest of the team risk averse. It clearly also made the customer uncomfortable, so I doubt we'll see her again.'

3. **Ask the boss's point of view.** For instance: 'Couldn't it have waited just a few minutes until we were in private?'

4. **Explain what would have been preferable.** For instance: 'Next time I, or one of the team, screws up, could you keep the reprimand private, please.'

5. **Outline the consequences.** Use the 'If... then' process to outline the positive consequences of the manager doing what you have asked, For instance: 'If you can issue the reprimand in private, then you are more likely to get people to work better or harder for you than if they feel belittled in public.'

COACHING SESSION 56

Manage your boss: strategies

For each of the following issues, write down how you would deal with it.

Issue	Strategy
1. My boss is cold and unsociable, seldom taking time to say hello and goodbye or smiling.	
2. My boss takes no human interest in my life; health, family, hobbies, weekend, holiday, etc.	

3. My boss is not clear what he/she expects of me in terms of my behaviour, outcomes and productivity.	
4. My boss doesn't care what my opinion is of things that relate to my work – such as what support I need, how my morale is, what suggestions I have.	
5. My boss often criticizes me or my work (or that of co-workers) in front of other people.	

6. My boss often gives credit to the wrong person, or to the team where it should go to an individual.	
7. My boss seldom notices when I do something right and just takes it for granted that it is what I'm paid for.	
8. My boss bears a grudge; he/she keeps reminding me of a mistake I made months/years ago.	

9. When something goes wrong, my boss is more interested allocating blame than putting it right.

10. In the event of a customer complaint, my boss always backs the customer and undermines me.

11. My boss is a very bad listener!

12. My boss has favourite(s) and whipping boys in the team.	
13. My boss is a follower of fashion, blindly adhering to the latest management 'fad'; consequently we are constantly bombarded with change initiatives.	
14. My boss allows some (or all) of the team to coast. Targets (if set) are easy to achieve; poor performance is tolerated.	

15. My boss takes the view that people beneath him/her are not employed for their brains. They should not think but simply do as they are told and follow the rules.

ONLINE RESOURCE

Manage your boss: strategies (sample completed exercise)

Download a completed exercise, with suggested strategies for each issue, from:

www.TYCoachbooks.com/Management

NEXT STEPS

There may be a genuine reason that you read this chapter with a large dose of salt – for instance, if you work in a very hierarchical organization where nothing you do will have the slightest effect on your boss's management style or behaviour. If that is the case, and it is a big 'if', then you are going to have to manage your *view* of the boss. You are going to have to accept that you can't change the situation, so you might as well just stop worrying about it or complaining about it (even if your complaints are never to the boss but just to the rest of the team, your partner or anyone else who will listen to you having a good old moan!). You might also like to consider that if you continue in this organization, you will probably turn into the same type of person that you are currently moaning about!

In the next chapter – our final one – we will look at how keeping abreast of your industry can contribute to your being an excellent manager and how knowing the value of your team can help you increase that value.

👍 TAKEAWAYS

What are the things you are going to do proactively, to generically manage your boss?

_____

_____

_____

_____

_____

_____

_____

_____

_____

What are the things you are going to do to pre-empt a specific behaviour from your boss that you know is going to create a problem when it happens?

_____

_____

_____

_____

_____

_____

_____

_____

_____

_____

What are the things that you are going to do on a reactive basis, when your boss does something that you can predict (based on your knowledge of your boss's 'usual' behaviour)?

_____

_____

_____

_____

_____

_____

_____

_____

What are the things that you are going to learn to just ignore?

_____

_____

_____

_____

_____

_____

_____

_____

_____

MINDING YOUR BUSINESS

16

OUTCOMES FROM THIS CHAPTER

- Test your knowledge of your industry and the legal standards relating to it.

- Use a diagnostic tool to work out the value of your team to your organization and thus be in a position to increase or – if it came to it – defend that value.

There are two elements to this topic:

1. minding your business

and...

2. minding your business!

MINDING YOUR BUSINESS (I)

In Chapter 7, number 9 and number 10 of the 'The key of the door to good management' were:

9. **Sector knowledge:** A good manager understands their industry so that they can answer questions and perform their work more effectively.

10. **Respect for the law:** Being a manager lays you open to all manner of responsibilities – health and safety, employment law, consumer rights, professional liability... the list is constantly changing. A good manager doesn't have to be a legal expert but an understanding of the basics and how/where to find the detail is important.

So here are two short 'tests' to help you assess how well you are performing in these two areas. Try to answer as honestly as you can.

COACHING SESSION 57

Your sector knowledge

What do I know of the history of the sector (over the last five years)?

_____

_____

_____

_____

_____

_____

What is the sector worth financially in our geographical market? What percentage of this market do we hold?

_____

_____

_____

_____

_____

_____

Who is the biggest player in terms of income, profit or market share in the sector?

_____

_____

_____

_____

_____

What different customers are there in the sector? Do we supply all the different customer groups? If not, why not?

_____

_____

_____

_____

_____

_____

What is the latest innovation in the sector? Are we in there at the leading edge?

_____

_____

_____

_____

Who is our biggest competitor?

_____

_____

_____

_____

_____

What is their USP (Unique Selling Proposition): what makes them special?

_____

_____

_____

_____

_____

What is the current forecast for the next 12 months in the sector with regard to growth?

_____

_____

_____

_____

_____

_____

What is the next big development in the sector with regard to new products or service?

_____

_____

_____

_____

_____

What is the current average rate of customer satisfaction in the sector? How does our level of customer satisfaction compare to the average?

_____

_____

_____

_____

_____

What is the single biggest threat to the sector at the moment?

_____

_____

_____

_____

_____

In how much detail could I explain (to an interested third party) the processes which we follow to provide our goods or services to our customers?

_____

_____

_____

_____

_____

_____

COACHING SESSION 58

Your legal knowledge

What generic (nationwide/global) laws directly affect our business?

_____

_____

_____

_____

_____

_____

What specific laws are there relating to our business?

_____

_____

_____

_____

_____

_____

What institutions exist in our country to regulate, promote and represent our business? What differentiates them from each other?

_____

_____

_____

_____

_____

_____

_____

What voluntary codes of conduct or standards do these institutions set above and beyond the laws of the land? To which of these institutions' codes do we (cl)aim to abide by?

_____

_____

_____

_____

_____

_____

_____

What qualifications are there which are directly relevant to our business and what overseas qualifications exist that are recognized as equivalents?

_____

_____

_____

_____

_____

_____

_____

How do I keep in touch with changes in law, voluntary codes and best practice? How do I keep my team up to date?

_____

_____

_____

_____

_____

_____

_____

_____

If you are a good manager you should have been able to answer all these questions in some considerable detail. If you are left with no response, or an educated guess, consider making a concerted effort to find a more detailed answer... soon.

MINDING YOUR BUSINESS (II)

Everyone has to be 'businesslike' in the twenty-first century, even if they aren't running a business. This section looks at the basic and universal 'rules' of businesslike efficiency to help you to protect your own career and the positions of your staff. It is a short section as you could be working in as diverse a career as direct door-to-door sales or brain surgery, the Special Air Service or the Mrs Tiggywinkle's Wildlife Rescue Centre. So it really boils down to a short diagnostic 'test'.

COACHING SESSION 59

You and your team's value

1. What is the annual cost, to the organization for which you work, of employing you and your team? Remember to factor in the elements below:

- everyone's salary

- employer's National Insurance contributions

- employer's pension contributions and all other benefits such as health care etc.

- your team's 'share' of the cost of the support functions of the organization such as HR, finance, facilities, etc. as well as the overhead cost of each of you having a desk, a phone, a PC, uniform, etc.

Total:

2. What is your team's annual contribution to the organization? This may be quite simple to calculate – for example: if you are a sales team, what is the total value of net sales that the team generates. Or it could be quite complex: how much is saved by your organization by employing your team of cleaners in comparison to outsourcing the cleaning to a third party, or using casual labour? Alternatively, the matter may be wrapped in moral, ethical and political considerations: what is a neonatal intensive care team worth to a region or nation? If soldiers aren't fighting, what value is the peace that their existence and credibility brings to the nation and the world?

Total:

Looking at the two totals, is there a clear, positive value that your team brings to the organization? If there is, then you have the data to form a benchmark of improvement and the arguments to protect and defend your team's existence. If there are clear numbers but no positive value, then your job and your team are on the endangered list.

For many managers, the simple answer is that they actually have no idea of the figure that should even be in the total box in Question 1. Not knowing that figure raises the question of how you will ever be able to improve the value you offer to the organization and its customers. It also means that you have little ability to forecast when the bean-counter's wicked glare will fall upon you and your team as a potentially expensive cost to the organization.

Armed with a strong and genuine knowledge of the cost vs. the benefit that you and your team provide you will have the raw materials to defend your common existence should the situation ever need it.

ACTION PLAN

That's it. You have read the book, so now you are a better, more rounded and more effective manager. Box ticked.

Well, not really. Now you have to live the life you planned in the early section about managing your career. You have to manage your own learning and development, having experiences and reflecting on them sensibly, developing yourself and your abilities. You have to build and rebuild your work team each time there is a change in their make-up or a change in their objective. You have to motivate them and manage their performance on a daily basis so that the image that they and other people have of you is enhanced. You have to strive to influence others and have a fulfilling career of achievement. You have to mind your business constantly and as consistently as you possibly can.

Use this space to write in your action plan for your development as a manager.

Keep this book to hand and dip into it regularly. Share it with members of your team and regularly repeat the coaching sessions in it. A coach is for life, not just for the couple of days it took you to get from the first page to the last.

Good luck!

Rus Slater

PS I am always happy to hear from people who have comments about my books. Feel free to offer any anecdotes, ask any questions or make any suggestions about this book. Now that we live in the interconnected world, you can easily find me online.

http://coach-and-courses.com/

HELP DESK

Below is a summary of the learning outcomes in this book. Use it as an aide-memoire to make sure that you are covering all the bases.

Introduction to management

- Begin to think about the nature of management.
- Understand the difference between leadership and management.
- Learn about the development of management as a discipline.

Managing yourself (I): aspiration and goal setting

- Understand your career aspirations.
- Assess your goal-setting management.
- Learn – or revise – common goal-setting techniques, including SMART.

Managing yourself (II): motivation

- Understand how to manage your motivation.
- Learn about the nature of proactivity and why it is so important.

Managing yourself (III): your 'personal brand' and how to develop it

- Understand the importance of your brand image.
- Learn how to develop your brand effectively.

Managing yourself (IV): your learning and development

- Learn about the different types of learning.
- Develop your own action plan for your learning goals.

Managing yourself (V): your morale

- Learn how to keep your morale on an even keel.

Managing others: introduction

- Reflect on the key questions of management.
- Learn about the 21 key qualities required by an excellent manager.
- Carry out self-assessment of your characteristics as a manager and – if you dare! – ask your team members to assess you.

Your day-to-day management activities

- Learn how to refocus more of your time on people management.
- Use a checklist to help you structure your people-oriented management activities.

Delegating successfully

- Learn about the barriers to delegation and how to overcome them.
- Understand why effective delegation is a core management skill.
- Develop an action plan for delegation.

Building and maintaining a team

- Learn about Tuckman's Stages of team formation.
- Understand how to manage team formation effectively.
- Understand the importance of maintaining team spirit or 'health' through active assessment.
- Try out some useful tools for building your team.

Managing your team members' development and performance

- Understand the value of managing your team members' development effectively, in terms of the individual, the team and the organization
- Learn how to manage team members' performance on an ongoing basis, not just once a year!
- Acquire some simple procedures for responding to team members' performance, both good and bad.

Managing a remote team

- Understand the particular requirements of managing a remote/virtual team.
- Draw up a communications management plan for a remote/virtual team.
- Consider appropriate communications technologies for managing a remote/virtual team.
- Learn how to maximize the team spirit of a remote/virtual team.

Managing motivation

- Consider and reassess your ideas about your team members' motivation.
- Understand the actual wide range of motivators that keep employees at work.

Managing other managers' people

- Learn how to maximize your negotiating skills.
- Understand how to use the logos–ethos–pathos paradigm to become an effective influencer.

Managing your boss

- Use a diagnostic tool to work out what kind of boss you have.
- Learn some simple techniques such as 'High 5' to manage your boss's more negative behaviours.

Minding your business

- Test your knowledge of your industry and the legal standards relating to it.
- Use a diagnostic tool to work out the value of your team to your organization and thus be in a position to increase or – if it came to it – defend that value.

INDEX